SOCIALIZATION GAMES
FOR MENTALLY RETARDED
ADOLESCENTS AND ADULTS

SOCIALIZATION GAMES

FOR MENTALLY RETARDED

ADOLESCENTS AND ADULTS

By

David Moxley

Nevalyn Nevil

Barbara Edmonson

CHARLES C THOMAS • PUBLISHER
Springfield • *Illinois* • *U.S.A.*

Published and Distributed Throughout the World by
CHARLES C THOMAS • PUBLISHER
2600 South First Street
Springfield, Illinois 62717, U.S.A.

©*1981, by* CHARLES C THOMAS • PUBLISHER
ISBN 0-398-04546-1
Library of Congress Catalog Card Number: 81-5601

*With THOMAS BOOKS careful attention is given to all details of manufacturing
and design. It is the Publisher's desire to present books that are satisfactory as to
their physical qualities and artistic possibilities and appropriate for their particular
use. THOMAS BOOKS will be true to those laws of quality that assure a good
name and good will.*

Library of Congress Cataloging in Publication Data

Moxley, David.
    Socialization games for mentally retarded adolescents and adults.

    Bibliography: p.
    Includes index.
    1. Mentally handicapped—Rehabilitation.   2. Socialization—Study
and teaching.   3. Educational games.
I. Nevil, Nevalyn.   II. Edmonson, Barbara.   III. Title.
HV3004.M65   616.85'8806   81-5601
                                                 AACR2
ISBN 0-398-04546-1

Printed in the United States of America
SC-RX-1

AUTHORS

David Moxley, M.S.W. is a Graduate Research Associate at The Nisonger Center for Developmental Disabilities of The Ohio State University. He is also a Consultant to the Childhood League Center, Columbus, Ohio.

Nevalyn Nevil, M.A. in psychology, is a Graduate Research Associate at The Nisonger Center for Developmental Disabilities of The Ohio State University. She is also a Consultant to the Association for Developmental Disabilities, Columbus, Ohio.

Barbara Edmonson, Ed.D. is Adjunct Associate Professor of Psychology, The Ohio State University, and former Director of Psychology Training at The Nisonger Center for Developmental Disabilities. She is Principal Investigator for the project "Development of an Innovational Program for Disturbed Retarded Institutional Residents."

PREFACE

The purpose of *Socialization Games for Mentally Retarded Adolescents and Adults* is to provide professional and nonprofessional personnel with a practical framework for encouraging positive social behavior from their clients. Although the socialization game approach was conceived of as a technique for working on institutional wards with persons who have severe behavior problems, the approach can be used in an array of programmatic environments. These include prevocational, vocational, day activity, educational and community residential programs. Thus, teachers, social workers, psychologists, vocational specialists and activity therapists as well as direct care workers, e.g., attendants, mental health technicians, and residential counselors, will find this book relevant to the habilitation of persons with deficits in social development.

The design of the book lends itself to the implementation of a socialization program. The first section introduces the socialization game approach. It provides an overview of the development of our approach, then a rationale for the use of socialization games and a discussion of their design. As our approach requires a group format, section two outlines specific considerations one should take into account when forming a group whose membership is mentally retarded. The third section is devoted to group leadership. This focuses on desirable characteristics of a group leader and examines the goals and tasks of group leadership. The last section includes a game assessment scheme that analyzes, along several dimensions, the seventy socialization games that are presented in this section. The assessment scheme will assist leaders in selecting games that are appropriate for members of their particular group.

We want to emphasize that it is not our intention to provide readers with a packaged approach to a socialization program. We hope that our concepts and ideas will blend usefully with the reader's own remedial ideas and plans. Through such collaboration we can realize more creative and practical ways of providing critical programming in the areas of socialization and social skill development.

Columbus, Ohio

December, 1980

ACKNOWLEDGMENTS

We gratefully acknowledge the support and assistance provided by a number of individuals who contributed substantially to the development of this manuscript. First and foremost, we extend our appreciation to the managerial staff of Forest Cottage: William "Corky" Campbell, Unit Manager, and Jack Beatty, Program Coordinator, who continuously provided the necessary support and encouragement enabling us to keep our groups virtually intact for over two years. We are also particularly indebted to many members of the direct care staff who actively supported our efforts through their enthusiastic participation in our groups. To our media specialist, Kathi Donini, we extend special recognition for the countless hours of videotaping and editing which provided us with process tapes of our group sessions. For the clerical and editorial expertise of our typist, Kathy Shaffer, whose patience never waned through the many revisions of our manuscript, we extend our grateful appreciation. Also, our gratitude is extended to John P. Bendekovic, Associate Professor of Social Work at The Ohio State University, who assisted us in developing our ideas about working with groups. Finally, we acknowledge the women of Forest Cottage, our group members, whose enduring interest and unique contributions made it all possible.

CONTENTS

SOCIALIZATION GAMES FOR MENTALLY RETARDED ADOLESCENTS AND ADULTS

SECTION 1

THE SOCIALIZATION GAME APPROACH

BACKGROUND

The socialization game approach evolved over a two-year period of work on two security wards of a state institution for the mentally retarded. Most of the thirty women who lived on these wards were in the moderate range of mental retardation; others, severely retarded. Almost all of the women had adequate levels of self-care skills but were characterized by high levels of aggressive and destructive behavior. Because of their severe difficulties in getting along with others they were, for the most part, excluded from off ward programming and were confined to their wards around the clock. Threats, insults, screaming, fighting, biting, and the destruction of property were frequent occurrences. Distrustful of interpersonal contact, many of the residents spent much of their time isolated in the corners of their wards or lying on their beds. Positive social interaction between the residents was rare. Occasions for positive group social interaction were rarely provided.

Conditions on the ward contributed to the atomistic behavior. Many of the women had long histories of institutionalization characterized by deprivation, inconsistent punishment and abuse. Overworked and undertrained aides lacked the motivation, knowledge, or the technical support to implement habilitative activities. A primary goal of the aides was to maintain control. They attempted this by keeping residents apart and isolated and by severe punishment for transgressions. A frequent punishment was to take a prized possession from a resident who may have broken a rule, or acted out. This would result in an outburst of rage, and a whole cycle of behavioral contagion would be set in motion. The punished resident would displace her anger onto someone lower in the pecking order and the displacement response would continue

3

until virtually every resident was involved in verbal or physical conflict. Some of the aides would show favoritism towards a resident, showering her with special privileges. As material resources were scarce, this special treatment often resulted in the favored resident's being physically attacked or provoked into attacking others through their harsh language and hostile gesturing. A strategy for an attempt at control was to use the most feared resident at the top of dominance hierarchy as an "enforcer," with the privilege of punishing others.

Because the residents of these wards were being managed through isolation, intimidation, and punishment, little warmth and few attachments existed between them. Lack of interpersonal trust pervaded the environment.

As a special project, to strengthen and supplement an innovational behavioral program (Edmonson, Moxley and Nevil, 1980; Moxley, Nevil and Edmonson, 1980; Edmonson, Nevil and Moxley, 1980; Nevil and Edmonson, 1980) we planned the socialization game activities with a goal of shaping positive interaction between peers, and with a secondary objective of improving the interactions between the direct care staff and the residents. In part this involved changing the negative valences that each person represented to the others into positive values. The methods we used via the games were basically those of desensitization, and of developing or strengthening social reinforcers such as attention and praise that could be used as contingencies for positive interpersonal behavior. Also, because of their years of depersonalization, games were used to make residents aware of their own attitudes and attributes in addition to those of others. Through trial of the games we invented, we discovered what was characteristic of the most successful, as described later in this section, and it became continually easier to design additional activities.

EPILOGUE

New resources enabled the ward administrator to attract more and more capable, direct-care staff to the cottage. A broader and more consistent program was developed and inservice training provided. Game groups were scheduled over a sixteen-month period on each ward either before or after supper once a week and they began to attract the on-duty aides as participants.

The overall effect of the program, the games in conjunction with the use of good behavior charts, merit badges for competencies, and other programming, was a marked decrease in social isolation and an increase in friendly and prosocial behavior. Consequent to the overall program, all of the residents have been accepted in off-ward programming, all have been able to earn grounds privileges by good behavior, and a number have been transferred to less restrictive environments. A third of the women have had referrals to community group homes.

WHY USE GAMES?

The games are effective at holding the interest and attention of participants while they try out a new behavioral repertoire. The laughter, the action, and the recognition that group members receive provide sufficient incentive to enable most individuals to learn to sit in a group, to wait for their turn, to try something new; later, to begin to assist the group leader, and to interact positively in the group with one another.

The games are useful in promoting peer interdependence when the leader, after giving a demonstration, encourages the members to direct or to help one another in subsequent trials. Certain games are designed to require mutual assistance from the participants.

In the games, players can be coached to better performance levels without their feeling they have failed at something. The warm and enthusiastic game leader, by focusing on the players' strengths and successes, helps to desensitize members to critical feedback. There are no right or wrong performances, but only better ways of playing. This aspect of the game procedure can have a carryover effect on the interactions between the staff and the residents in other situations. Generalization is, of course, more likely when other members of the staff join the leader and a group of retarded persons in the games. Then, the leader's example and the experience of positive interactions between the staff and residents does tend to carry over to other situations. Through playing the games the staff becomes more aware of socialization goals and their importance. Staff are encouraged to relate to the retarded individuals as peers rather than as subordinates. Because the participants have had a good time together, their liking for one another is strengthened.

CHARACTERISTICS OF THE GAMES

As is more fully described in Section 5, the games focus on five socialization goal areas. The most basic set, "Interpersonal Distance" games, encourages group members to interact with close proximity. This socialization area is important in helping people with behavior problems learn to tolerate closeness to people whom they have not trusted in the past. In one of these games, "Blow Round," participants sit closely together around a table in order to keep a ping pong ball from being blown off the table by others.

Another set of games has the goal of "Knowing About Yourself." In these games group members learn to know their own feelings; learn how others make them feel; and are encouraged to make independent choices and decisions. As an example, "I Feel Really Good About . . ." requires participants to decide whether they feel good or bad in reaction to different situations.

A third set of games has the goal of members' gaining knowledge about others. Several of these games, for example, require a participant to learn physical characteristics of other members, or certain preferences of their peers and their peers' feelings or attitudes. The game "I Know Something About You" requires participants, in turn, to respond to questions about the dress and/or physical characteristics of others while they are blindfolded.

A fourth set of games focuses on prosocial behavior such as sharing, cooperation, helping, and mutual problem solving. For example, in "I Have a Problem — How Can You Help?" participants are presented with another's problem and must decide how to help.

The fifth set of games promotes social competence, the ability to engage in rule-governed and appropriate social behaviors, and to solve problems. Games in this category teach participants how to greet others, ways of dealing with anger, asking for help, and dressing in a socially normative manner."Something's Wrong with those Clothes" teaches participants to discriminate what is inappropriate due to misfit, soil, or need for repair. Participants then suggest ways of making the clothing look "OK." Some games in this category are used to develop problem solving by members who have the necessary communicative and cognitive ability. Games such as "The Problem Box" involve members in considering problems that often occur in their environments—having something stolen, something lost, or something that needs repair. In some settings a member may have problems with money, loss of a job, jealousy over a friend. Certain of these games let members think of alternative ways of dealing with the problems.

The games lend themselves to many situations and purposes. After one has identified a socialization goal area, one can seek appropriate games in the scheme on pages 42–53. If necessary, games can be modified to fit particular persons or groups, or new games invented. While many of our games overlap goal areas, a primary goal should be evident in their design.

Many moderately and severely retarded individuals have short attention spans, are distractible and have either high or unusually low activity levels. Many have difficulty in processing verbal instructions, especially if they contain more than one command. They are often hesitant to try something new, perhaps because their failures have been emphasized more than their successes. Our socialization games, therefore, have been designed in terms of the following criteria:

SIMPLICITY. Verbal explanations are minimized. Rules are usually communicable through modeling and imitation.

NOVELTY. Games frequently employ props, e.g., a blindfold, or stimulus cards, that can be used by group members, and which introduce an element of novelty.

SHORT DURATION. Games move at a quick pace and the short duration prevents satiation and tends to hold attention.

PARTICIPATION. Each group member is given a role that keeps him or her active. For example, if two members are playing a game in the middle of the group circle, other members have roles that may include counting, directing, or expressing an opinion about what is going on in the middle.

TURN-TAKING. Each game includes a turn-taking procedure

to insure that each member will have an opportunity to participate during the session. This reduces competition over who is to have the next turn.

Success and Recognition. Social recognition is provided by the leader and other members for attempts to participate, for following the rules, completing steps of the activity, trying appropriate new strategies, and helping other members; thus a participant has many opportunities to feel successful.

Cost. Games are designed to keep material cost and leader preparation time to a minimum. Many games require no materials. Most materials can be found among household articles as with "Helping My Neighbor Find Her Stuff" or are quickly made according to the directions in the game instructions.

Each game description includes the title, the materials needed, the procedure, including participant selection procedures. The games are organized according to the group life phase and the socialization goal area to which they pertain. Under the heading, Materials Needed, instructions are provided for any stimulus materials. Game procedures are simply stated and often include recommendations to guide the leader. A recommended member selection method is indicated (methods are reviewed in Section 4) after the description of the game procedure. With certain games there are additional suggestions for adapting or modifying the game.

The games can be used over and over again with different outcomes. Repetition seems to enhance effectiveness and interest value. As members become more familiar with the procedure, they can concentrate less on the rules and more on varying the outcome or their responses. Most games can be modified so the level of skill required to succeed can be gradually increased or adapted to fit the skill level of group members. Some of the games indicate advanced levels or second versions that require more skill. Most games can be easily adapted by the game leader to reduce or increase the level of difficulty. In the game "Find the Person" a simplified adaptation might require a participant to identify which of two persons has the object shown on the stimulus card. In an advanced version, members might be asked to classify or identify everyone in the group who has the object shown on the card. The leader should regard games as models or examples, and should experiment with modifications that are addressed to the socialization needs of the group members.

RELEVANT POPULATIONS AND
PROGRAMMATIC ENVIRONMENTS

The socialization games can be used with adolescents and adults in a variety of programs and environments. Although our games were designed for an especially difficult population of moderately and severely retarded residents in an institution, they have been used with more mildly retarded men and women in a community group home and with adolescents in a public school classroom for educable mentally retarded. The objectives of the games are relevant to the personal adjustment programs in prevocational or vocational workshops, and useful as recreational or leisure activities in community group homes, day activity centers and institutional dormitories. The games, and modifications of them, would make good activity supplements for a special education social skills curriculum.

Reference to the scheme on pages 42–53 should suggest the relevance of particular games to certain groups. Furthermore, the classification system should help a programmer identify some areas of habilitation need. After trial of the games designed for those areas, the group programmer or the game leader may think of modifications or new games that would be relevant.

SECTION 2

ORGANIZATIONAL AND
ENVIRONMENTAL REQUIREMENTS

A socialization game program involves the use of a group format. Thus when developing a game program the group leader
should be aware of factors that influence the behavior of a group.
This chapter refers to important variables of group organization
and physical environment that can affect group cohesiveness and
behavior.

GROUP ORGANIZATION

Group organization is important to the outcome of the
game program, as the group's organization will influence the
ability of members to form interpersonal ties and to work coop-
eratively within the group.

Although there is little research literature on the development
of cohesion among group members who are retarded, field trials
of our games have shown an increase in friendly interactions and a
decrease in unfriendly behavior consequent to the group experience (Han, 1980). Variables of group organization include: (1) the
composition of the group; (2) the size of the group; (3) the basic
rules for participation in the group; (4) the zones of participation
in the group; (5) the length of a group session; and (6) the use of a
time-limited group program. These are discussed below.

Composition

The question of *who* participates in a socialization game
group may not be an option for a group leader whose clientele
consists of retarded persons in a residential unit. In such an
instance, the leader may have to work with an intact group consisting
not only of individuals of all levels of retardation, but also perhaps of persons of different ages, and different levels of physical

10

disability and behavioral adjustment. Although such diversity makes group leadership difficult and decreases the habilitative impact of the games, this should not dissuade one from developing a game program. Some of the socialization games described in the final section of this book can be utilized with heterogeneous groups.

If a leader can select specific persons to become members of a socialization game group, we suggest that he consider the following criteria:

(1) The sex of members is a significant variable of group composition. Many of the games can be utilized with same-sex or heterosexual groups. If a goal is to promote heterosexual interaction, then a group balanced with males and females should be developed. Same-sex groups might be considered when clients withdraw from members of the opposite sex; act out or become aggressive around members of the opposite sex; or need to develop peer interaction skills with members of their own gender.

(2) The age of group members is another important variable. Although our experience has shown that the socialization games appeal to a broad age range of persons who are retarded, a narrow age range may promote more group cohesion, because of members' similar developmental interests. A narrow age range may thus contribute to a group leader's goal of promoting peer relationships among group members.

(3) The admixture of members of different levels of retardation is an important variable. Our own experience has shown that a broad range of abilities, e.g. several members who are mildly retarded and several members who are severely retarded, creates problems for the group leader, because it is difficult to modify any single game so that it will sustain the interest and involvement of group members of widely discrepant abilities. In such an instance, the more able may be bored, or the least able virtually excluded from active involvement in group process. However, a group of persons of different levels of retardation within a narrow range can function with positive results. For example, for several months we conducted a group of institutional residents of moderate and severe levels of retardation in which the members with moderate retardation were able to act as peer models and coaches for the

severely retarded members. The latter gained much by observing the behavior of their more capable peers and the more capable were rewarded by their coaching role. A group leader may therefore want to seed his group with several persons who are functioning at a higher level than most group members. The caveat here is that the disparity in levels of retardation between group members should not be too great.

(4) Other variables that should be considered by the leader are the nature and extent of members' physical and behavioral disorders. Physical disability should not be cause for exclusion from the group, but the group leader must be sensitive to individuals' limitations and make adaptations in order to facilitate participation.

(5) Behavior disorders are apt to be more problematic than physical disabilities to the leader who tries to achieve balanced group composition. The person who acts out aggressively toward others should not be allowed to jeopardize the safety of others. On the other hand, because many of the games are designed to promote positive social behavior, one should not routinely and rigidly exclude people who act-out, as they need opportunities to acquire more adaptive social skills. When persons with seriously maladaptive behavior are included, the leader must set limits, and must find ways of holding their interest to promote a progressive decline in disruptive behavior.

(6) Another variable affecting group organization is the participation in the group by direct care staff. When we lead groups in an institutional setting we encourage participation by hospital aides. The residents often have positive attachments to aides, and participation by these aides makes the group session even more important and enjoyable to the residents. Another plus is that through their participation in groups, the direct care staff may become more aware of the habilitative goals of the sessions and this may promote more positive interaction between them and the residents.

To summarize, differences in group composition can have a profound effect on the behavior and attitude of individual members, and leaders should be aware of the characteristics of members that differentially influence the functioning of groups. If leaders have the option of selecting members they should plan in terms of the following variables: (1) sex; (2) age; (3) level of retardation; (4) physical disability; (5) behavior disorders; and (6) the possible inclusion of members of the direct care staff. If the leader does not have control over these variables then he or she should consider how the characteristics of group members may affect group process.

Size

Group size should vary according to whether one or two group leaders are involved, and according to the behavior problems presented by individual group members. We have found the decision matrix presented in Figure 1 to be useful in planning the size of the group.

Level of Behavior Problems

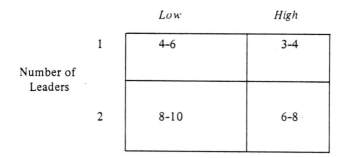

Figure 1. Decision matrix for planning size of game group.

The cells indicate the number of members that we recommend in relation to the number of leaders and the incidence of behavior problems presented by the group. When one leader is working with a group with a low incidence of behavior problems, a range of from four to six clients is suggested while a range of from three to four members is suggested for a group with a high incidence of maladaptive behavior. When two leaders are involved, a group with a low incidence of behavior problems may range in number from eight to ten members. For a group with a high incidence of behavior problems six to eight members are suggested.

The size of the group and the decision whether to have two leaders should be influenced by the level of retardation of group members and the nature of any physical and behavioral disabilities presented by group members. Given two good leaders and clients with a low incidence of maladaptive behavior, an ideal size is from eight to ten members.

Basic Rules for Participation

Another organizational variable consists of the basic rules for group participation. These rules should be announced to the group, or discussed with the group at the onset of the socialization game program. Rules might include: (1) no hostile teasing; (2) no threats; and (3) no bringing of edibles to the group. Leaders would remind the group member who violated a rule that it was not permissible; and would think in terms of defusing a difficult situation and carrying on with the game activity rather than thinking of punishment or expulsion. The goal is to preserve the group and maintain the interest and cooperation of members. Exclusion may become necessary, if several verbal reminders about rules have been ineffective.

Zones of Participation

We conceive of two zones of participation as constituting another aspect of the organization of a group. The first zone or the "core group," are the members, seated in a circle, who are involved in face-to-face interaction in the group. The second zone, the "outfield," consists of those who sit or stand on the fringe or edge of the group and watch the activity of the core members. We have observed that some persons, because of negativism or aversion to physical proximity, resist becoming involved in the core group. We encourage such persons to sit nearby and watch. From time to time the leaders are able to get the individuals to respond to a question or participate, even if briefly, with the core group. This participation, vicarious or direct, by reluctant persons should be encouraged as it can lead to learning and to eventual core group participation.

Length of A Group Session

Sessions should be structured to take into account members' attention spans. The length of a session is a critical factor in maintaining good interaction within the group. Once group members become bored or otherwise inattentive, positive interaction decreases and some members may withdraw from the group or begin to act-out. During our pilot program it appeared that an optimal session ranged from 30 to 45 minutes. This time span was sufficient for "getting ready," a game, and "cooling down."

Time-Limited Programming

This final organizational variable involves planning for the life-span of the group. Time-limited programming is an option for group leaders such as psychologists, activity therapists, and teachers who must provide programming to a large number of clients for a limited period of time. Short-term game groups might range in duration from 10 to 20 sessions. Examples of time-limited groups are the following: (1) providing new group home residents an opportunity to become acquainted with one another; (2) intervening when residents are having difficulty interacting with one another; (3) promoting a person's adaptation to new programming, e.g., adjustment to a new prevocational workshop; and (4) providing socialization programming when professional and paraprofessional manpower is scarce.

GROUP ENVIRONMENT

The physical environment is influential in maintaining the organization of the game group. Variables that should be considered by the group leader include: (1) characteristics of the room; (2) environmental distractions; (3) type of furniture and its arrangement; (4) useful "props;" and (5) scheduling group time.

Characteristics of the Game Room

The room should be large enough to accommodate the group sitting in a circle formation. For some games additional space may be needed. Ideally, the space utilized for socialization games should not be overly large. If space in a ward must be utilized, the game area boundaries should be clearly denoted with tables or screens or chairs.

The most important guideline is that the same room or meeting area be used each time. The familiar setting helps members remember the procedural rules, and pleasurable experiences there create within members an expectation of pleasure that optimizes attentiveness and effort.

Controlling Environmental Distractors

A group leader wants members to focus their attention on what is happening within the core group. Factors that divert attention from group involvement include large windows; noise from television, radios, or record players; nonparticipant staff members entering and leaving the room; nonparticipant clients laughing, running or tantruming; and extremes of room temperature. Distractors can often be prevented or minimized. The group leader's plan to control the environment should help to maintain good group interaction.

Type of Furniture and its Arrangement

Because the games are intended to increase physical and social contact between members, the furniture that is used is important. Couches and sofas encourage members to sit next to one another, but there should be comfortable (and movable) chairs for those who avoid physical proximity. Group participants might sit on the floor on overstuffed pillows, but remember that members with physical disabilities or poor motor control may be handicapped by this arrangement. The important consideration is to use furniture that will be comfortable for the duration of the group session.

A good arrangement of furniture is an open-ended circle (see Figure 2). This allows props, e.g., a small table to be moved in and out of the group with minimal disruption of group activity, while allowing members to conveniently move in and out of the center of the circle as required by certain games.

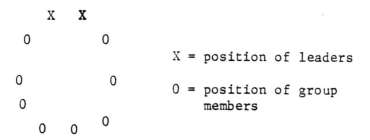

Figure 2. Arrangement of furniture for group session.

Use of Props

Many of the socialization games require props. These may
be extra chairs, a table, pillows, or floor markings which are made
with masking tape. In order to avoid disruption of the group,
these props should be set up or moved to the periphery of the
group before beginning the game session.

Scheduling Group Time

In scheduling group games, leaders should choose a time that
does not conflict with meals and responsibilities, e.g., school,
chores, work, field trips. Finally, once a time is selected, the leader
should maintain this as the regular group time. This will give
members some predictability about when the group will be held.
Members will become secure and confident that their group will
be held at a set time during the week.

An optimal time in the institution where we tested our games
was early evening just before or soon after dinner. Evening hours
for institutional residents are often void of any organized pleasurable activity. Game groups are especially enjoyable and valuable
on weekends in institutional settings, when there are few other
habilitative activities.

SECTION 3

GROUP LEADERSHIP

The role of the group leader is a challenging and often demanding job but is certainly not limited to those with extensive training or expertise. Leadership and effective group management skills develop from the experience one gains by actually conducting groups. It is important then to "take the plunge" and start working with a group on the assumption that you, as the leader, will grow with the group members. The focus of this section is on group leadership: leadership characteristics, leadership goals and general techniques, and the tasks of the group leader, including many specific techniques for promoting group involvement and cohesion.

GENERAL CHARACTERISTICS OF A GROUP LEADER

The leader should be aware of certain leadership characteristics or behaviors that appear to be necessary for effective group management. These are to: (1) demonstrate enthusiasm, (2) convey warmth, (3) communicate effectively, and (4) promote trust.

DEMONSTRATE ENTHUSIASM. The group leader is a powerful role model for group members. Members will not only model or imitate what the leader explains and demonstrates, but will also model the mood he or she conveys. It is thus essential for the leader to express enthusiasm and interest in the group activities. If not, the members' interest will decline. The leader creates the mood and sets the tone for group activities. A principle is to be as enthusiastic about the activities as you expect your members to be. It is often helpful to emphasize and even exaggerate your interest both verbally, and nonverbally with gestures. We have clients who initially felt that the games were childish or foolish but who discovered they were fun in reaction to our enthusiasm. The group leader increases the interest value of the games by partici-

18

pating as a peer rather than as a "parental" type of leader.

WARMTH. The leader must convey warmth, acceptance and recognition. Warmth and concern are conveyed through verbal statements, body language, and through facial expression and physical gestures. Warmth is expressed in many ways but includes such gestures as greeting, and, if necessary, shaking hands with each member, praising individuals and the group as a whole for their performance, and showing special consideration for members' problems or concerns. While the group game session is not group therapy designed to solve members' personal problems, a sensitive and warm leader should give special attention to members with special needs, and encourage others in the group to provide support. We have found that if a member is upset before a group session but made to feel accepted and needed by the group and leader, he/she will often have a change of mood and will forget about the upsetting situation. Thus, the group session can be an effective redirection technique to promote positive feelings toward self and others.

COMMUNICATION. Effective communication is essential in establishing and maintaining groups. The leader must be highly conscious of his/her language—both verbal and body language—and of the receptive and comprehending abilities of group members. An initial step is to determine the members' levels of understanding through questions and trial activities.

Then, when introducing the game materials, the leader should use a combination of verbal instructions and physical modeling, to be repeated as necessary. For members who appear unable to follow lengthy verbal instructions, instructions may have to be broken down into simple steps, and each step rehearsed or walked through before proceeding on to the next. Simplification of instruction, and repetition, are important techniques of the group leader.

TRUST. The group leader can be an effective facilitator of positive interactions only if he/she has earned the members' trust. Trust is promoted when groups are conducted regularly on a certain day at a set time. Group members need to learn to expect the session and feel secure with their expectations. It is also important that the leader consistently enforces the rules. Rules for acceptable conduct were made for the benefit of the group and need to be followed if the leader is to be trusted and effective.

As a model, the leader can make mistakes intentionally to show members that "It is OK to make a mistake." This model of human fallibility lessens members' concerns about mistakes and failure, thereby reducing performance pressure.

LEADERSHIP GOALS AND GENERAL TECHNIQUES

The group leader's primary role is to teach members positive means of interacting with one another. When members learn to interact positively with one another in the group without being prompted to do so by the leader, the likelihood is increased that such behaviors will transfer to situations outside of the group. Han's data (1980) supports the group game approach as she found that significantly more friendly interactions occurred immediately following the group games than after a variety of other structured group activities.

With many newly organized groups, a first goal of the leader will be to teach members to listen and to sit in a group formation. In the beginning phase of group involvement, the leader must be highly didactic, reinforcing, and intrusive in order to establish the basic rules for participation. As the members learn to play their roles and follow the rules, the leader increases the members' responsibility by assuming a less directive posture. Gradually, the leader works toward the group members' helping one another.

To increase individual responsibility and enhance the attraction of the group, the leader must know what behaviors to reinforce and how to reinforce them. Two major categories of behavior that should be reinforced are positive social interaction and self-directed behavior. Positive social interaction includes cooperative behaviors such as sitting quietly and waiting for a turn, following the group rules, and members' helping one another or praising one another for their efforts. The leader can promote positive interaction by offering members opportunities to help him or her and to help other members. Through shaping simple forms of positive interaction with praise, smiles, and occasional touching, a members' social repertoire can be developed to a self-directed level. At this level, members no longer wait for requests from the leader, but, for example, sit quietly and follow the rules. They may begin to offer assistance spontaneously and initiate other positive interactions.

Reinforcement preferably consists of verbal and nonverbal recognition and praise. Recognition and praise of group members' efforts should consistently come from the leader, but can be even more effective when coming from the group. The leader teaches members to "recognize" and reinforce one another. We demonstrate praise by hand clapping for good performance. Group members first follow the leader's cue and eventually discriminate appropriate reinforcement times without relying on the leader's cue. Verbal praise follows a similar course, as, initially, group members imitate the leader and then spontaneously praise others. Teaching members to look for and publicly recognize the efforts of others promotes growth from an egocentric perspective to higher level social awareness. Some of our most egocentric members have learned to look beyond themselves and exhibit genuine excitement over the successes of others. We have seen one such member pat another on the back and exclaim, "I'm so proud of you."

Mutually helpful and self-directed behavior should be goals of the group leader and it will require conscious effort to foster the members' reliance on peers and on self rather than on the leader. One technique is to redirect members who need assistance to peers, rather than responding to these needs. Members can also be encouraged to solve their own problems by using graduated prompting. With this technique, rather than solving a problem, the leader prompts an answer or suitable response with a series of questions intended to carry the individual through the steps to a suitable response. Prompts can be gestures, verbal cues or leading questions.

To promote goals of peer helpfulness and self-directed behavior, the leader should allow members to direct themselves as much as they can and will. When the leader must intercede, his method of intrusion is important. His or her attempts should be to guide via prompting, insofar as feasible, rather than by a direct demonstration or a full explanation. If a member cannot recall what it is that he is supposed to be doing, or has difficulty with the activity, the leader can prompt the procedural steps. For example, if Linda has not been able to locate the group member with a design that matches her own for the "Match Game," the leader might first ask Linda and then the group, "Did you/she look at everyone's design?" The leader prompts the group to respond with "No"or a headshake. The leader could then ask another member to help Linda walk around the group and as the pair stops at each member, the leader could guide with questions; e.g., "Did you look at Mary's?" "Does yours look like Mary's?" and so on. The leader could encourage the peer helper and others to assist with additional questions as necessary. In this way, the leader encourages both problem-solving and peer assistance.

Group members are also prompted to give assistance to members with situations that are unrelated to specific game activities. For example, if a member has a physical disability that limits his involvement or mobility, others are encouraged to assist but not to *do* the activity for that member. Even individuals with severely limiting conditions can assist others in some way, and it is the responsibility of the group leader to encourage the contributions and assistance of each member based on his/her individual ability. Every member should discover that he can be a valuable contributing asset to the group.

Group leaders should encourage members to generate their own ideas. For instance, during the "Greeting Game," members are encouraged to come up with their own examples of "weird" and "OK" behaviors.* We have found that members functioning in the low-moderate to severe range of mental retardation are often able to come up with their own idea with prompting. If a member can give an example of "weird" or "OK" behaviors, he or she is becoming able to discriminate between behaviors.

TASKS OF THE GROUP LEADER

Planning for Phases of Group Life

Groups begin; grow with respect to planned goals; and then end. To accommodate these three identifiable phases of group life, games have been designed to address the needs specific to each phase, which we refer to as the Warm-Up Phase, the Game Phase

---

*We credit Rosen, Clark and Kivitz (1977) and Rosen and Hoffman (1975) for the use of these terms in behaviorial discrimination training.

and the Termination Phase.

Warm-Up Phase

With beginning groups made up of members who lack basic group skills, or groups with low-moderate to severely retarded members, the emphasis is on getting members interested and enthused about the group experience and teaching basic group skills. The leader focuses on the fun value of the game while teaching members to sit in a group, maintain attention, follow directions, respect rules, and take turns. Games designed for the Warm-Up Phase are action-oriented and require imitative responses rather than more advanced cognitive skills.

The leader gauges the readiness of group members to move on to the Game Phase by observing their interest level and group-skill level. Depending upon the duration of the group and the needs of group members, the leader decides when the group is able to handle games addressing specific socialization goal areas. Some groups, meeting for a short duration with members who are severely socially maladaptive, may remain in the Warm-Up Phase until termination. Group leaders are encouraged to try games in the interpersonal distance goal area as these games tend to promote a fairly high degree of member involvement. Also, some warm-up games address the area of knowing about others. These games are especially useful for beginning groups as they encourage members to learn each others' names. The important point is that members' behavior will tell the leader whether the phase or particular game is appropriate.

Game Phase

The majority of the games are designed to improve skills in the five general socialization areas detailed in Section 2 (knowing about yourself, knowing about others, interpersonal distance, prosocial behavior and social competence). In general, these games place more cognitive demand on members and require the ability to remain seated and wait for a turn because only one or two can play at a time.

Most groups should spend the bulk of their sessions in the Game Phase working on goals prioritized by the leader to meet the needs of the group members. As games within each socialization area represent a range of difficulty levels, a leader may want to concentrate on a particular goal area before moving on to another. For example, a leader may focus on decreasing interpersonal distance through relevant games before moving on to games promoting knowledge about others or social competency.

Leaders should not, however, feel confined to a single socialization area and may instead want to rotate games among the socialization areas. Again, the critical task for the leader is to select games that meet the needs and skill levels of group members.

Termination Phase

The Termination Phase of group life is designed to provide a positive group ending to the group experience so that members will feel less wary about their involvement in future groups. All too often, groups simply stop with an announcement at the final session; or, even worse, members discover after the fact that their group has been discontinued. Members are then left with no understanding as to the reason for the termination and may be left with a multitude of negative feelings such as anger, sadness, rejection or personal inadequacy. We feel that a sensitive leader *must* consider the feelings of members about their group and in so doing prepare members for the conclusion of the experience. Whether the group is time-limited or ongoing, termination is inevitable. The important aspect is that termination procedures be planned and implemented prior to the final session to permit leaders and members some time to work through their feelings and adjust to the ending of the group.

The games that are appropriate for the termination phase are designed to sensitize group members to the approaching ending of the game program. Termination games provide participants with opportunities to express their feelings and attitudes about the end of the group experience. Some games help members plan for alternative activities. Although members may not become involved in such activities, these games communicate the leader's concern that members continue interacting with one another even though the game program has ended.

We recommend that the leader arrange the time frame so that

the group begins the termination process three sessions prior to the final session. For groups with members who have poor communication skills, the leader can adapt the model by omitting the first session. The recommended model outline follows:

SESSION I. Prior to playing the game members are involved in a discussion to think about and to express their feelings about the group. The leader may facilitate discussion with structured questions such as:

- What is your favorite game?
- What do you like best about our group?
- Are there any things you don't like about the group?

Each member is given the opportunity to respond to questions about the group. The leader then announces that group will meet two more times, and provides members with an explanation for the ending of the group. If the group was time-limited the leader may remind the members weekly "This is our 5th/6th/7th group, we will meet 10/9/8 more times." Then, termination becomes the final part of the countdown. For open-ended groups however, the leader needs to explain to members the reason for the group coming to a close. It may be that the leader is giving others an opportunity to participate in a group or that the leader is changing roles or jobs. Whatever the reason, members should be informed and given the opportunity to react. Members also need to know the leader's feelings about the group and the impending termination. The session then becomes an exchange of feelings and attitudes between leaders and members.

SESSION II. This part of the termination process consists of a termination ritual, or the playing of games designed to facilitate movement towards closure. The games provide a structured format for expression of feelings and attitudes about the group and games. The leader reminds members that the following session will be the last group session.

SESSION III. The final session includes both a group ritual and group product. Members are asked to select a piece of construction paper and crayon. Members then make a card for another group member selected by drawing a name or picture. Each member is then asked to shake hands or hug the selected member before giving him or her the card. The session is concluded with the leader presenting his/her card to the group. If possible, leaders might also take pictures of the group for each member to keep as a concrete reminder of the group experience.

If realistic, leaders may also tell members that even though the group will no longer be meeting, the leaders will be back to establish contact from time to time. It is important that a leader attempt to minimize members' feelings of rejection by assuring members of his/her caring for them and desire to remain in contact.

Planning the Group Session

Each group session may be divided into three parts: (1) "Getting Ready," (2) "Game Time," and (3) "Cool Down." For a 30-45 minute game session we suggest 5 minutes for Part 1, 20-30 minutes for Part 2 and 5-10 minutes for Part 3. The duration of phases should be determined by the number of players, their interest, and their habilitative needs.

"Getting Ready" permits leaders to promote group identity using some of the suggested techniques and prepare members for the game. The leader may want to remind members of the group rules and procedures that will be used during the game session. For example, a leader might hold up a prop and elicit from members the rules regarding its use. Also, group member responsibilities such as being a peer helper or in charge of rearranging the furniture could be delegated.

Once the attention of members has been sustained through "Getting Ready," the leader shifts into "Game Time" in which the leader introduces the game through a modeling demonstration and all members have opportunities to play as suggested in sections titled "Phases of Group Life" and "Introduction of the Games."

"Cool Down" is a time in which to reinforce members for their participation. During the final round of a game, the last person or persons to participate would be given the honor of dispensing the reward (pretzel, finger food). Members are thus rewarded by special recognition for awaiting their turn. It is also important to provide closure to the session without a letdown. The leader tells group members that they have done a great job and worked together as a good group. Members could clap for each other's efforts and should be reminded of their next group meeting time.

A leader may also want to involve all members in an activity to provide closure to the game session. One technique is the group vote. The leader asks, "Everyone who liked playing *(name of game)*, raise your hand. If you would like to play it again, raise your hand." Group members can assist by counting the hands. The "vote" method encourages members to state a preference and recognize differences in preferences. When the activity is repeated, the leader should remind members, "We are playing *(name of game)* again because the group chose to play it." Thus, the group members are shown that their preferences or choices within the group are meaningful and important.

Preparing Members for Game Sessions

While groups may be conducted "at a moment's notice," there are many advantages to scheduling them at regular times. Groups scheduled to occur on a specific day at a certain time promote an awareness of time. When members expect the session as a regularly occurring event they can anticipate and prepare for it, thus becoming more self-directed and ready for responsible participation behavior.

The program staff prepares members by reminding them of the day and time of their session at intervals during the week and several minutes before the group is scheduled to begin. As an example, a staff member can say, "Your group meets Tuesdays at 5:30," or "Your group will meet in 10 minutes." To remind members ahead of time rather than to command their participation at the time of the sessions, allows them to assume the responsibility for being ready.

Getting People to the Group

For residents who appear disinterested and for those who actively refuse to participate in the group, a follow-up prompting procedure is often effective. The following 3-step procedure must be approached positively:

1. The leader or a staff person says, "We would like you to come to the group."

2. The individual is reminded that he/she is important to the group. For example, "You do (could do) such a good job. We really need you to help us in the group." The message is that the member has a lot to offer and is needed by the other group members.
3. If the individual refuses, he/she is told, "When you are ready to come to the games, you may join us."

Some members respond well to being given a special job or an assisting role as an incentive for coming to the group. This procedure should be used only a few times to permit that person to have some successful experiences. The assisting role can then be rotated to others. It is the leader's responsibility to make the group rewarding enough to maintain the members' interest. We have found that most members will continue to attend once they have participated in a good session.

It is important that the group begin on time with or without all members. While the member who initially refuses to attend may join at any time, he/she must see that the group will not wait. Individuals usually do not like to be excluded for long from activities that are fun for others.

Introduction of Games

The leader introduces a game by demonstration. We have developed a four-step modeling strategy for introducing group games:

(1) The leader introduces the game by announcing its name and simple concrete instructions for playing. If materials are involved, the leader may want to acquaint the members with them using a questioning procedure. For example, if a blindfold is used, the leader can ask group members if they can identify the object and then encourage a member to demonstrate its use.
(2) The leader "walks through" the steps.
(3) The leader selects a member and uses prompting to begin the game.
(4) Group members play the game with the facilitators providing direct guidance and prompting.

Once a game has been played by the group, it can usually be reintroduced by presenting the materials and basic rules. Through questioning, the leader can determine the extent of members' recall and can adapt the procedures accordingly. With repetition, the members learn the games and can provide assistance as peer facilitators.

Maintaining Formation of the Group

Many strategies are used by the leader to maintain the attention and interest of the group members. Close circular arrangement of the chairs or cushions promotes proximity of the members and facilitates attention to one another. The activities are designed to promote active involvement of group members so that they will want to remain in the group. Most important, however, are the skills and techniques of the group leader in maintaining group cohesion.

The effective group leader has the dual role of "planner" and "scanner." As a "planner," the leader must organize and direct the activities so as to permit the active involvement of all members. In addition, the leader must be a "scanner" throughout the group sessions for situations that threaten to disrupt the group process, and follow through with planned intervention techniques. The leader can maximize group cohesion and prevent disruptions by using the following techniques:

TURN TAKING. Let members know that they will have a turn to participate. One method of turn taking is called "blind selection." Members' names or pictures are put into a box from which a member draws to determine who has the next turn. This method gives everyone an equal chance of being selected; it eliminates favoritism and maintains the attention of group members through anticipation of being next.

Another selection procedure is for the leader to select a member from those who are competing with raised hands for a turn. The advantage of this selection method lies in the control the leader maintains over the group. Members who are distracted or disturbed may be selected and thus redirected to the activity when necessary.

While a selection procedure is recommended for each individual game, the procedure may often be varied.

HOLDING ATTENTION. Attention focused too long on a single member can often result in losing the rest of the members. The leader can maintain the attention of all group members by switching his/her focus from member to member, or by rotating attention around the group.

It is important that the flow of reciprocal interactions from leader to member to leader to another member, be maintained to keep all members interested and involved throughout the session.

PARADOXICAL PROMPTING. To increase members' attending behavior and facilitate active participatory learning, we often present a verbal paradox or false statement to group members. A paradoxical statement may be a misstatement of group rules such as, "If we stand up, we will get a pretzel when the bell rings," or game procedure, "The blindfold goes over the mouth." The purpose of such statements is to encourage members' active listening and correction of the statement rather than blind acceptance of leader's remarks. As members learn to respond appropriately to leader's statements, the leader is also able to gauge the members' comprehension of game rules and procedures.

Shaping members' discrimination of false statements requires that the leader encourage members to listen carefully to repetition of the statements and actively guide members through questioning to recognize the inaccuracy. Initially, our members required considerable prompting to challenge leader statements. With practice and improved listening skills however, members learned to discriminate the false statements. Often, members respond immediately to our false statements with a resounding "No" followed by a corrected version.

MAINTAINING FOCUS ON ACTIVITY. Group members may want to talk about personal needs or concerns for which the group session is not the appropriate time or place. The effective leader uses redirection techniques. Consequently, when Linda begins to talk about the money she was given, the leader can respond with, "Linda, we're talking about (or playing) a game right now. You may talk about that after the group."

TOUCH CONTROL. Touch control consists of patting an arm or the back of a member as praise or reinforcement for staying in the group. Through appropriate touching, the group leader can communicate acceptance, support, or praise for a job well done. The leader using touch control is also a social model demonstrating acceptable touching to group members. Again, as with use of the leader's attention, touching should be rotated among group members.

RECOGNITION OF COOPERATIVE BEHAVIOR. The leader can promote group process by reinforcing the group for working together. It is important to give verbal recognition and support to members for cooperative behavior with such statements as "Everyone works together so well in this group," or "You are all doing a great job together," or "See how we can help each other." Group members should be encouraged to assist each other on an individual basis and to provide group support by clapping and cheering for others' efforts. The message is that the group is a supportive team and that each member contributes to the group's activity.

PROMOTING GROUP IDENTITY. A major task for the leader is to promote "we" feelings among group members or a sense of group togetherness. Members need to see themselves and the other members as forming a distinct group that is identifiable from other groups in terms of purpose and expectations. Beyond identifying one's membership in a given group, members need to feel positive about their roles if the group experience is to exert any influence on them. There is much evidence to show that the more attractive a group is to the members, the greater the positive influence members and leaders will have on one another.

Groups acquire an identity and positive valence, or attractiveness through the efforts of the leader. Most basically, the leader promotes the identity of the group by designating a set time, place and membership composition. Members then learn that they and some of their peers are part of a regularly occurring special event different from other daily group activities.

The unique identity of the group primarily comes from the nature of the activities. Members need to know why they are coming to the group and what is expected of them as members. Giving the group a name such as "Game Group" enhances group identity by giving members a common label reflecting the purpose of the group. We begin and conclude our groups with a ritual in which the leader asks all members of the "Game Group" to stand up. The leader then questions members, "What is the name of our group?," "What do we do in our group?," and "When do we meet?" As members learn to verbalize (or sign) together the name, activity and day their group meets, they tend to feel a greater sense of belongingness and identification with each other as members of the same group.

Concrete symbols such as the signal bell and timer may also serve to promote group identity as they represent unique procedures specific to the group activities. Posters made by the group members and leader with the group name, a picture of group members and each member's contribution also reminds members, between sessions, of *their* group.

Group members express their feelings about the group basically through their willingness to participate in the group activities. Other indicators of members' perception of group identity are member's questions and comments about the group between sessions. One of our groups gathers together before each session without prompting and talks among themselves and to staff about their group activities. In addition, two members of the same group who chose to move to a more desirable location asked the direct care staff if they could return for the "game group."

TANGIBLE REINFORCEMENT. It may be helpful to use a tangible reinforcement to teach members to sit and remain in a group. A simple method is to use a kitchen timer set on a variable interval schedule. Members are taught that when the bell rings they will receive a treat only if they are seated. We have found small stick pretzels to be an effective inexpensive reinforcer. In the beginning, arrange for reinforcement on a short interval basis, perhaps an average reinforcement interval of 2-3 minutes. Gradually, the intervals are increased as members adapt to the group rules. This procedure also promotes peer facilitation as members may be given the responsibility of dispensing the reward to the group.

MINIMIZING DISTRACTORS. A high noise level can be very disruptive to the group process. We have used two cueing methods for quieting loud groups. The signaling bell used for initiating the group may also serve as a cue to stop talking and listen to the leader. A leader's finger to lips with an accompanying "ssh," or an explanation "When my finger is up, our lips shut," can be used to teach group members to respond to the leader's control. Members of one of our groups who had a hard time controlling their talking were taught to cover their mouths with a hand when cued by the leader. In time, group members can assume the responsibility of monitoring and controlling the noise level.

The leader must also be able to maintain or regain the attention of group members who are obviously distracted or upset. The leader must be an active "scanner" to note members who seem frustrated or upset. Quick intervention using redirection techniques is often effective at diverting the upset member. Often a positive comment or question about the individual's performance is sufficient. Another method is to assign the member a specific task. One of our most disruptive individuals who constantly threatened and assaulted other members responded more appropriately when given the role of pretzel dispenser, contingent on her appropriate cooperative behavior.

If group members are involved as helpers throughout the session behavior management problems are reduced. When they are busy, they are more interested and less apt to feel frustrated. Not all members will respond at all times to redirection. If a member is losing control and disrupting the group, we suggest a three step warning procedure. First, the individual is told, "You are disturbing the group," and given an opportunity to gain control of her behavior. If the behavior persists, the member is warned of the contingency, "If you are not quiet, you will have to leave." Finally, if the behavior continues, the individual is told, "You must leave the group, but you may come back when you have calmed down." Failure to comply results in a physically prompted escort away from the group. It is important to remind the member that when he or she has calmed down he/she can rejoin the group. He/she is not being punished, but being given an opportunity to get his/her behavior under control. The guiding principle for ruling on inappropriate behavior is: How much can the group tolerate and still remain intact? If the behavior is distracting to others, removal of a disruptive individual could be presented as a group decision for the benefit of members who want to participate.

Attention of group members may also wane if an activity is too complicated or if an activity is overly used. The leader views the group's mood and behavior as a barometer of the interest value of a specific game. When signs of group boredom or satiation occur, the leader should be prepared to modify the activity or switch to a different activity.

Co-Leadership

A helpful strategy is to enlist the assistance of a co-leader. Two individuals, working as a team, are especially helpful with clients who exhibit severe behavior problems.

While co-leaders will necessarily overlap in terms of their respon-sibilities, direction of the games and managing behavior represent two different roles. One co-leader can be primarily responsible for directing the game while the other can assume primary responsibility for group maintenance and behavior management techniques as was discussed above. The leaders maintain an unobtrusive communication dialogue mostly on a nonverbal basis so that each can supplement and assist the other. It is important that the leaders agree with one another in their communication with group members.

The co-leader approach will probably be necessary for clients with severe behavioral problems as some clients require almost one-to-one contact to become adapted to the group. As an example, in one of our groups a new member initially spent most of her time wandering around trying to grab things from other members. It required the skillful efforts of one leader to shape her sitting behavior and to prompt her participation while the co-leader kept the game going with the other members. Once members learn to follow the group rules, it is possible to fade one co-leader and continue the group with a single leader.

Not all group leaders, of course, have the option of a co-leader. If one is to work by oneself with the clients who display serious behavior problems, a careful assessment of the characteristics of the members and the limitations of a single group leader is in order as indicated in Section 2. Strategies include limiting the size of the group and selecting adaptive peers as models and helpers.

This section was developed to prepare individuals to become more effective group leaders by orienting them to their roles and providing helpful suggestions and strategies for maximizing group cohesion and member growth. Prospective leaders should view the facilitation strategies as procedures which have been found to be useful with some groups but which should be adapted to meet the needs of particular group members. Leaders are urged to use these techniques as the basis for the development of their own strategies.

SECTION 4

SOCIALIZATION GAMES

This section describes seventy socialization games and outlines the materials and procedures for playing each game. The games are arranged in terms of five socialization areas: interpersonal distance, knowing about yourself, knowing about others, prosocial behavior, and social competence. They are coded in terms of a game assessment scheme to indicate the competencies that are required of the participants, the focus of rewards, the degree of psychological risk taking, and group involvement, whether the game is appropriate for the beginning phase of a group or the middle or the terminal sessions of group life, as explained in Section 3, and the amount of preparation time and materials that are necessary.

THE GAME ASSESSMENT SCHEME

The game assessment scheme* is designed to help the leader make a good match between the requirements of a game and the characteristics of the group. To select a game, one scans the left margin of the assessment scheme to note the features. A group leader should examine and compare the characteristics of group members with each game feature that is being inspected. For example, when examining the feature of "functional competencies" the group leader may informally assess his group members in terms of their level of verbal communication. If many members have difficulty in verbal expression, then a game that is low in this feature should be chosen. Thus, the game assessment scheme is a guide for making a decision about whether a specific game should be used with a particular group.

While it is easier to select games for a more homogeneous

---

*A prototype of the assessment scheme was used by Bendekovic (1971) in comparing and contrasting an array of structured group activities.

group, or a group in which members have similar skill levels, one may not have the opportunity of working with such a group. To provide for the interest and success of all members of a heterogeneous group requires planning and thoughtful selection of game activities by the leader. A workable approach at times is to select games based on the abilities of the less skilled individuals and provide for the higher skilled individuals by giving them assisting roles.

At other times one can select games requiring slightly more complex skills and, again, the higher skilled individuals would be encouraged to assist the lower skilled members through the game activity. For example, in the game "Find the Button," lower skilled individuals in some of our groups were able to label and recognize the button but were often unable to think of a good hiding place, or, to look for the button with a systematic approach. Higher skilled individuals were asked to help these members hide the button in less visible places; and escort them around the group to demonstrate a systematic approach.

Six primary features are identified via the game assessment scheme: (1) socialization area, (2) competence needed, (3) focus of rewards, (4) psychological risks, (5) group aspects, and (6) administration. Each of these features and their subcharacteristics are discussed below.

1. *Socialization Area.* This term refers to the goal of each game. Some games have more than one socialization purpose, but they are here described in terms of the goal that seems primary.

2. *Competence Needed.* This is a term for the skills that are required of participants. These include the levels of verbal communication, motor behavior, and cognition that individuals need in order to participate successfully in the game.

> VERBAL COMMUNICATION. *Low* verbal communication games can be played by group members who are nonverbal. *High* verbal communication games require that most members be able to communicate verbally with others in the group. The game "Do This" is low in verbal communication as is "Stare Down," as they require only motor imitation. The game "I Like You Because . . ." is high in verbal communi-

cation because it requires members to state what they like about other group members.

MOTOR BEHAVIOR. Some games can be utilized with people who are *low* in mobility—for example, persons with severe motor problems. *High* mobility games require group members to leave their seats and move about. "Who's Talking" is a low mobility game as group members sit and listen to a tape recorder and try to guess which group member is talking. In "We Have A Lot in Common" members must move from station to station as various characteristics or attributes are named by the leader. For example, everyone wearing glasses is told to move to a specific area in the room.

COGNITIVE DEMAND. This feature refers to the cognitive skills demanded by the game. While cognitive demand is related to rule complexity, it specifically refers to the sophistication of the behavior required by the games. *Low* cognitive demand games require only simple imitation. Games *high* in cognitive demand may require role play, modeling or analysis of a problem and generation of solutions. "Putting on the T-Shirts" places a low cognitive demand on members as they are only required to put a T-Shirt on another member and members may learn their performance by imitation. "What Am I Doing" is a high cognitive demand game because members must enact situations and problem solve.

3. *Focus of Rewards.* The group procedure suggested in Section Three emphasizes that social rewards be disbursed throughout the group session. However, the games vary in terms of the focus of rewards that are suggested. Some games provide rewards to individual participants. Other games provide rewards to all group members at the same time. As an incentive for certain individuals, leaders may want to select a game that provides tangible rewards to individuals. However, in order to develop group spirit the leader may choose a game in which rewards are provided contingent upon the group's performance. The "to whom" dimension of the reward feature shows whether the reward goes to an *individual* or to the *group*. The reward feature of "Blow Round" is a tangible payoff to the group. If group

members can maintain a ping pong ball on a table top by blowing it away from the edge for a specified time period, e.g., one minute, then all group members receive an edible. Alternatively, other games such as "I Have a Problem—How Can You Help?" provide for individual rewards. The member with the problem and the member who provides the solution are rewarded individually for their efforts.

4. *Psychological Risks.* Leaders experienced in group work realize that group participation may expose members to criticism, embarrassment, or ridicule from others. Some of the games ask members to disclose their feelings, preferences, and even fantasies. The psychological risk factor inherent in self-disclosure may make some group members uncomfortable when initially playing some games. Games that require no self-disclosure are labelled *low*, and those which do call for self-disclosure are labelled *high* risk. "Find the Person" is low in psychological risk because members are not asked to reveal personal information. "Let Me Tell You How I'm Feeling Today" is a game high in psychological risk because group members must disclose and share how they feel about certain situations.

5. *Group Aspects.* Group aspects consists of two dimensions, *involvement* and *phase of group development.*

INVOLVEMENT. This is the extent to which the game promotes simultaneous involvement of all group members or, conversely, involves only one or two members at a time. *Low* involvement means that one or two members are active at a time. *High* involvement means that all or most group members are involved at one time. "Blow Round" is an example of a high involvement game.

PHASES OF GROUP DEVELOPMENT. This dimension indicates whether a game is appropriate for the *warm-up phase*, the *game phase*, or the *termination phase* of group life as explained in Section 3. During the warm-up phase, the leader is focusing primarily on teaching members to maintain attention, follow directions, respect rules, sit in a group and take turns. Games appropriate to the warm-up phase are usually action oriented, simple, and *high* in member involvement. These games promote interest and enthusiasm in the group while helping the members develop basic group skills. Games appropriate for the game phase generally place more cognitive demand on members and may be less action oriented. Lastly, the games that are appropriate for the termination phase of the group alert members to the approaching completion of the group program and allow them to gain closure to the group experiences. This dimension enables a group leader to select games that he/she feels are appropriate to the phase of group life.

6. *Administration.* Group leaders may not have access to funds to secure supplies or time to invest in lengthy preparation and planning for a group session. Two features, *materials* and *preparation/planning*, have been included to facilitate game selection.

MATERIALS. The supplies that are needed are listed on each game sheet under "materials." Games *low* in materials require few props. "Find Your Friend" is an example of a game which is low on this dimension. The game requires only a blindfold in addition to the standard set of pictures* of group members. Games that are *high* in materials require a number of props or materials. For instance, the game "Do We Go Together?" requires a number of personal or household articles.

PREPARATION/PLANNING. This refers to the amount of preparation required. Planning and preparation can involve planning for role play situations, making stimulus cards, or obtaining props and other materials. *Low* planning and preparation means that little time is required in order to implement the game. The game "Back to Back" requires no props and little preparation and planning. *High* planning and preparation means that the leader must spend some time developing materials or planning specific problem situations, role plays or scenes to implement the game. An example of a game demanding high planning and preparation is "Find the Person," as the materials include stimulus cards.

---

*A set of photographs of group members is used in many games and is an initial expense which is not considered in the rating of a game as either low or high with respect to the *materials* feature.

Standard set of photographs

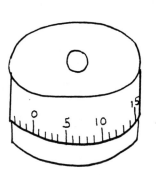

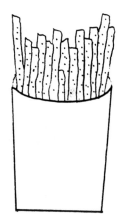

Timer

Edible
(pretzels)

Figure 3. Basic game supplies.

GAME ASSESSMENT SCHEME						
GAME TITLE	Blow Round	Do This	Don't Drop The Can	Guess Who	Hidden Object	I Wish
SOCIALIZATION GOALS	Inter-personal Distance	Inter-personal Distance	Inter-personal Distance	Inter-personal Distance	Inter-personal Distance	Inter-personal Distance
COMPETENCE NEEDED Verbal	Low	Low	Low	Low	High	High
Motor	High	High	High	High	Low	Low
Cognitive Demand	Low	Low	Low	Low	High	High
FOCUS OF REWARDS	Group	Group	Individual	Individual	Individual	Group
PSYCHOLOGICAL RISK	Low	Low	Low	Low	Low	High
GROUP ASPECTS Involvement	High	High	Low	Low	High	High
Phases of Group Development	Warm-up	Warm-up	Warm-up	Warm-up and Game Phase	Game Phase	Game Phase
ADMINISTRATION Materials	Low	Low	Low	Low	High	Low
Preparation & Planning	Low	Low	Low	Low	High	Low

GAME ASSESSMENT SCHEME						
GAME TITLE ·	Imitation Chain	Leading A Friend	Make Me Laugh	Mystery Object	Shape Match	Stare Down
SOCIALIZATION GOALS	Inter-personal Distance	Inter-personal Distance	Inter-personal Distance	Inter-personal Distance	Inter-personal Distance	Inter-personal Distance
COMPETENCE NEEDED Verbal	Low	Low	Low	Low	Low	Low
Motor	High	High	Low	Low	High	Low
Cognitive Demand	Low	Low	High	Low	Low	High
FOCUS OF REWARDS	Group	Individual	Individual	Individual	Individual	Individual
PSYCHOLOGICAL RISK	Low	Low	High	Low	Low	Low
GROUP ASPECTS Involvement	High	Low	Low	Low	High	Low
Phases of Group Development	Warm-up	Warm-up	Warm-up	Game Phase	Game Phase	Warm-up and Game Phase
ADMINISTRATION Materials	Low	Low	Low	High	High	Low
Preparation & Planning	Low	Low	Low	High	High	Low

GAME ASSESSMENT SCHEME						
GAME TITLE	Trading T-Shirts	Where's the Button	Which Hand?	Working Together To Beat the Clock	Are You Happy or Are You Mad?	Feelings About Our Group
SOCIALIZATION GOALS	Inter-personal Distance	Inter-personal Distance	Inter-personal Distance	Inter-personal Distance	Knowing About Yourself	Knowing About Yourself
COMPETENCE NEEDED Verbal	Low	Low	Low	Low	Low	Low
Motor	High (Upper Body)	High	High	High (Upper Body)	Low	Low
Cognitive Demand	Low	High	High	Low	High	High
FOCUS OF REWARDS	Individual	Individual	Individual	Group	Individual	Individual
PSYCHOLOGICAL RISKS	Low	Low	Low	Low	High	High
GROUP ASPECTS Involvement	High	High	Low	High	High	Low
Phases of Group Development	Warm-up	Warm-up and Game Phase	Game Phase	Warm-up	Game Phase	Termination Phase
ADMINISTRATION Materials	Low	Low	Low	High	High	High
Preparation & Planning	Low	Low	Low	High	High	High

GAME ASSESSMENT SCHEME						
GAME TITLE	Finish the Sentence	Here's How I'm Feeling Today	Honk If You Know I	I Feel Really Good About . . .	My Favorite Things	Name Warm-up
SOCIALIZATION GOALS	Knowing About Yourself	Knowing About Yourself	Knowing About Yourself	Knowing About Yourself	Knowing About Yourself	Knowing About Yourself
COMPETENCE NEEDED Verbal	High	Low	High	High	High	High
Motor	Low	High	Low	Low	Low	Low
Cognitive Demand	High	High	High	High	High	High
FOCUS OF REWARDS	Individual	Individual	Individual	Individual	Group	Individual
PSYCHOLOGICAL RISKS	High	High	High	High	High	High
GROUP ASPECTS Involvement	Game Phase	Game Phase	Game Phase	Game Phase	Game Phase	Warm-up Phase
Phases of Group Development	Low	Low	Low	Low	Low	Low
ADMINISTRATION Materials	Low	Low	Low	Low	Low	Low
Preparation & Planning						

GAME ASSESSMENT SCHEME						
GAME TITLE	Stand Up If You Agree	The Feeling Meter	Things We Like To Do Together	Back-to-Back	Can You Pretend?	Clothing Color Match
SOCIALIZATION GOALS	Knowing About Yourself	Knowing About Yourself	Knowing About Yourself	Knowing About Others	Knowing About Others	Knowing About Others
COMPETENCE NEEDED Verbal	Low	High	Low	High	Low	Low
Motor	High	Low	Low	Low	High	High
Cognitive Demand	High	High	Low	High	High	Low
FOCUS OF REWARDS	Group	Individual	Group	Individual	Individual	Individual
PSYCHOLOGICAL RISKS	High	High	Low	Low	High	Low
GROUP ASPECTS Involvement	High	Low	High	Low	High	Low
Phases of Group Development	Game Phase	Game Phase	Termination Phase	Game Phase	Game Phase	Game Phase
ADMINISTRATION Materials	Low	High	High	Low	Low	High
Preparation & Planning	Low	High	High	Low	Low	High

GAME ASSESSMENT SCHEME						
GAME TITLE	Find the Owner	Find Your Friend	Find the Person	Honk If You Know II	I Know Something About You	If I Were a Staff Member
SOCIALIZATION GOALS	Knowing About Others	Knowing About Others	Knowing About Others	Knowing About Others	Knowing About Others	Knowing About Others
COMPETENCE NEEDED Verbal	Low	Low	Low	High	High	Low
Motor	High	High	High	Low	Low	High
Cognitive Demand	High	Low	Low	High	High	High
FOCUS OF REWARDS	Individual	Individual	Individual	Individual	Individual	Individual
PSYCHOLOGICAL RISKS	Low	Low	Low	High	Low	Low
GROUP ASPECTS Involvement	Low	High	Low	High	Low	Low
Phases of Group Development	Game Phase	Game Phase	Game Phase	Game Phase	Game Phase	Game Phase
ADMINISTRATION Materials	High	Low	High	Low	Low	Low
Preparation & Planning	High	Low	High	Low	Low	Low

GAME ASSESSMENT SCHEME						
GAME TITLE	Name Draw	Name Game I	Name Game II	Pick a Friend	Put on the Thinkin' Cap	The Blindfold Game
SOCIALIZATION GOALS	Knowing About Others	Knowing About Others	Knowing About Others	Knowing About Others	Knowing About Others	Knowing About Others
COMPETENCE NEEDED Verbal	High	Low	Low	High	High	Low
Motor	High	High	High	Low	Low	Low
Cognitive Demand	High	Low	Low	High	High	Low
FOCUS OF REWARDS	Individual	Group	Group	Individual	Individual	Individual
PSYCHOLOGICAL RISKS	Low	Low	Low	Low	Low	Low
GROUP ASPECTS Involvement	Low	High	High	High	Low	Low
Phases of Group Development	Warm-up Phase	Warm-up Phase	Warm-up Phase	Game Phase	Game Phase	Game Phase
ADMINISTRATION Materials	Low	Low	Low	Low	Low	Low
Preparation & Planning	Low	Low	Low	Low	Low	Low

GAME ASSESSMENT SCHEME						
GAME TITLE	TV Star	We Had a Great Group!	We Have A Lot in Common	Whisper	Who Am I Talking About?	Who Is This Person?
SOCIALIZATION GOALS	Knowing About Others	Knowing About Others	Knowing About Others	Knowing About Others	Knowing About Others	Knowing About Others
COMPETENCE NEEDED Verbal	High	Low	Low	Low	High	Low
Motor	Low	Low	High	High	Low	Low
Cognitive Demand	High	High	Low	Low	High	Low
FOCUS OF REWARDS	Individual	Individual	Group	Individual	Group	Group
PSYCHOLOGICAL RISKS	Low	Low	High	Low	High	Low
GROUP ASPECTS Involvement	High	High	High	Low	High	High
Phases of Group Development	Game Phase	Termination Phase	Game Phase	Game Phase	Game Phase	Game Phase
ADMINISTRATION Materials	High	High	Low	Low	Low	Low
Preparation & Planning	High	High	Low	Low	Low	Low

GAME ASSESSMENT SCHEME						
GAME TITLE	Who's Missing?	Who's Talking?	Friendship Chain	Helping Each Other	Helping My Friend Find His/Her Stuff	Helping My Neighbor-I
SOCIALIZATION GOALS	Knowing About Others	Knowing About Others	Prosocial Behavior	Prosocial Behavior	Prosocial Behavior	Prosocial Behavior
COMPETENCE NEEDED Verbal	Low	High	High	Low	Low	Low
Motor	Low	Low	High	High	High	High
Cognitive Demand	High	High	High	Low	Low	Low
FOCUS OF REWARDS	Individual	Individual	Individual	Individual	Individual	Individual
PSYCHOLOGICAL RISKS	Low	Low	High	Low	Low	Low
GROUP ASPECTS Involvement	High	High	High	Low	High	High
Phases of Group Development	Game Phase	Game Phase	Game Phase	Game Phase	Game Phase	Game Phase
ADMINISTRATION Materials	Low	High	Low	High	High	High
Preparation & Planning	Low	High	Low	High	High	High

GAME ASSESSMENT SCHEME						
GAME TITLE	Helping My Neighbor II	I Have a Problem. How Can You Help?	The Magic Box I	The Magic Box II	Being Responsible I	Being Responsible II
SOCIALIZATION GOALS	Prosocial Behavior	Prosocial Behavior	Prosocial Behavior	Prosocial Behavior	Social Competence	Social Competence
COMPETENCE NEEDED Verbal	High	Low	Low	Low	Low	High
Motor	Low	High	Low	High	Low	Low
Cognitive Demand	High	High	Low	High	High	High
FOCUS OF REWARDS	Individual	Individual	Individual	Individual	Group	Individual
PSYCHOLOGICAL RISKS	High	Low	Low	High	High	High
GROUP ASPECTS Involvement	High	Low	Low	Low	High	Low
Phases of Group Development	Game Phase		Game Phase	Game Phase	Game Phase	Game Phase
ADMINISTRATION Materials	Low	Low	High	High	High	Low
Preparation & Planning	Low	Low	High	High	High	High

GAME ASSESSMENT SCHEME						
GAME TITLE	Don't Lose Your Cool I	Don't Lose Your Cool II	Mix and Match	Planning for Comfort	Should I Ask for Help?	Something's Wrong with Those Clothes!
SOCIALIZATION GOALS	Social Competence	Social Competence	Social Competence	Social Competence	Social Competence	Social Competence
COMPETENCE NEEDED Verbal	Low	High	Low	Low	Low	Low
Motor	Low	Low	High	High	Low	High
Cognitive Demand	Low	High	High	High	High	High
FOCUS OF REWARDS	Individual	Individual	Individual	Individual	Individual	Individual
PSYCHOLOGICAL RISKS	High	High	Low	Low	High	Low
GROUP ASPECTS Involvement	High	High	High	High	Low	High
Phases of Group Development	Game Phase	Game Phase	Game Phase	Game Phase	Game Phase	Game Phase
ADMINISTRATION Materials	Low	Low	High	High	High	High
Preparation & Planning	Low	Low	High	High	High	High

GAME ASSESSMENT SCHEME						
GAME TITLE	The Greeting Game	What Am I Doing?	What Am I Dressed For?	Who Can Help?		
SOCIALIZATION GOALS	Social Competence	Social Competence	Social Competence	Social Competence		
COMPETENCE NEEDED Verbal	Low	Low	Low	Low		
Motor	High	High	High	Low		
Cognitive Demand	High	High	High	High		
FOCUS OF REWARDS	Individual	Individual	Individual	Individual		
PSYCHOLOGICAL RISKS	High	Low	Low	Low		
GROUP ASPECTS Involvement	High	High	High	Low		
Phases of Group Development	Game Phase	Game Phase	Game Phase	Game Phase		
ADMINISTRATION Materials	Low	Low	High	High		
Preparation & Planning	High	High	High	High		

INTERPERSONAL DISTANCE

"Blow Round"

"Do This..."

"Don't Drop the Can"

"Guess Who"

"Hidden Object"

"I Wish"

"Imitation Chain"

"Leading a Friend"

"Make Me Laugh"

"Mystery Object"

"Shape Match"

"Stare Down"

"Trading T-Shirts"

"Where's the Button?"

"Which Hand?"

"Working Together to Beat the Clock"

TITLE: "Blow Round"

SOCIALIZATION
GOAL AREA: Interpersonal Distance

MATERIALS: Table, chairs, ping pong ball, timer

GAME PROCEDURE: Group members are seated around the table and instructed to place their chins close to the table. The leader then rolls a ping pong ball onto the table and tells the members to try to blow it over to the other side of the table.* Throughout the game, members are told to keep the ball in motion. If the group is able to keep the ball on the table until the timer buzzes, all members are awarded a pretzel.

PARTICIPATION
PROCEDURE: All group members are involved in this activity.

SUGGESTIONS: One way to develop group cohesion is to gradually increase the length of time required for the reward.

TITLE: "Do This..."

SOCIALIZATION
GOAL AREA: Interpersonal Distance

MATERIALS: No special materials needed

GAME PROCEDURE: Members are introduced to the cue "Do This" which means to imitate the behavior of the leader (in the fashion of "Simon Says"). The participants are instructed by the leader to "Do what I do when I say 'Do This'." Types of imitative responses that can be used in this game follow:

1. Body level of imitation: identifying/

---

*A timer is set for 30 seconds.

touching body parts, e.g., touching head, nose, mouth.

2. Verbal level of imitation: vocalizations or verbalizations e.g., Hi!, Boo!

3. Feeling level of imitation: mood and feelings, e.g., anger, sadness, happiness.

PARTICIPATION
PROCEDURE: Everyone in group has a chance to participate at the same time.

SUGGESTIONS: The leader may want to ask whether a group member wants to be the leader for a round of "Do This." It is possible that the member may have to be prompted in providing a response to be imitated. To do this, the leader may whisper a suggestion to the leader of the round.

TITLE: "Don't Drop the Can"

SOCIALIZATION
GOAL AREA: Interpersonal Distance

MATERIALS: Coffee can, board that is approximately 3 feet long and 4 inches wide, edible

GAME PROCEDURE: Starting and finishing points are marked on the floor with masking tape or objects.* Two group members are placed at the starting point and each given an end of the board with the coffee can placed in the center. The members are asked to help each other take the can to the finish line without dropping it. If members are able to get to the finish marker with no more than one drop of the can, an edible is earned.

PARTICIPATION
PROCEDURE: Two members at a time are selected by

_____

*Approximately 25 feet apart.

the BLIND SELECTION METHOD.
(see page 29)

SUGGESTIONS: To make the game more challenging the leader can partially fill the can with water.

TITLE: "Guess Who"

SOCIALIZATION
GOAL AREA: Interpersonal Distance

MATERIALS: No special materials are required

GAME PROCEDURE: One member sits with his/her back to the group. The group members are seated in a semi-circle. Another member quietly walks up behind the seated member and puts hands over his/her eyes asking "Guess Who?" The seated member then must guess who is behind him/her.

PARTICIPATION
PROCEDURE: The BLIND SELECTION METHOD is used.

TITLE: "Hidden Object"

SOCIALIZATION
GOAL AREA: Interpersonal Distance

MATERIALS: Small box, blindfold, familiar items (at least 1 per member) (see "Mystery Object")

GAME PROCEDURE: One member is blindfolded. Another member takes an object and hides it under a small box. The blindfold is removed and the member must guess what the object is with clues provided by the other members. Leaders can prompt group with questions like: What color is it?, How big is it?, Do you wear it?, Where do you keep it?, What do you do with it?, etc.

PARTICIPATION
PROCEDURE: The BLIND SELECTION METHOD is used with the member hiding the object becoming the next to be blindfolded.

TITLE: "I Wish"·

SOCIALIZATION
GOAL AREA: Interpersonal Distance

MATERIALS: No special materials are required

GAME PROCEDURE: A member thinks of a wish (with assistance of the leader). The member whispers it to the person next to him/her and he/she passes it on. The wish is passed on until it gets to the person seated next to the one who started it. This person then announces the wish to the group. The person who started it then tells his/her wish to the group.

PARTICIPATION
PROCEDURE: Group members can take turns in order or the BLIND SELECTION METHOD can be used.

SUGGESTIONS: The leader may have to act as a "bridge" in getting a message from one group member to another. However, the leader should only intervene when a group member is having difficulty in attending or has communication problems.

TITLE: "Imitation Chain"

SOCIALIZATION
GOAL AREA: Interpersonal Distance

MATERIALS: No special materials are required

GAME PROCEDURE: The leader initiates a gross motor act to

the group member on his/her right (arm waving, tapping head, clapping hands, etc.). The member is instructed to pass the act to his/her right, with each member continuing to pass the act until it comes back to the leader. The member to the right of the leader is then instructed to pass his/her own different activity around the circle.

PARTICIPATION
PROCEDURE: The LEADER SELECTION METHOD (page 29) is used, in terms of the ordering of members in the circle, until all have had a turn.

TITLE: "Leading A Friend"

SOCIALIZATION
GOAL AREA: Interpersonal Distance

MATERIALS: Rolled up socks, tangible reward

GAME PROCEDURE: Starting and finishing points are marked on the floor with tape or objects.* Two members are told that a sock will be placed between their arms and that they must help each other by holding their arms tightly together. The members are instructed to walk from the start to the finish marker without dropping the socks. If members are able to reach the finish line with no more than one drop, they earn a reward.

PARTICIPATION
PROCEDURE: Two members at a time are selected by the BLIND SELECTION METHOD.

---

*Placed approximately 25 feet apart.

TITLE: "Make Me Laugh"

SOCIALIZATION
GOAL AREA: Interpersonal Distance

MATERIALS: No special materials are required

GAME PROCEDURE: Two group members sit across from one another. One group member takes the role of "being silly." The "silly" member makes a face or a funny movement and attempts to make his partner "crack up" (laugh). The partner tries to keep from laughing. However, when the partner does laugh, the members switch roles.

PARTICIPATION
PROCEDURE: Two group members at a time are selected by the BLIND SELECTION METHOD.

SUGGESTIONS: The group member who is taking the role of "being silly" may need prompts to make the other laugh. The leader can go through a three step procedure of prompts. First, the leader can say to the member, "Make a funny face." If this doesn't work, the leader should try a concrete verbal suggestion like "Make a face like a monkey." Finally, if this doesn't work, the leader can model a funny face to the member and ask him/her to imitate it.

TITLE: "Mystery Object"

SOCIALIZATION
GOAL AREA: Interpersonal Distance

MATERIALS: Box of familiar objects, e.g., brush, scissors, spoon, cup, glasses, toothbrush, and a blindfold

GAME PROCEDURE: One member is blindfolded. Another

member selects an item from the box and presents it to the blindfolded member for identification. Clues as to the use of the object may serve as prompts.

PARTICIPATION
PROCEDURE: The BLIND SELECTION METHOD is used to select group members. The member presenting the object then becomes the next blindfolded member.

TITLE: "Shape Match"

SOCIALIZATION
GOAL AREA: Interpersonal Distance

MATERIALS: Two small boxes or containers, two sets of matching shapes, e.g., circle, triangle, square, cross, heart, star, diamond, etc., blindfold

GAME PROCEDURE: Each set of shapes is put into a box or small container. Each member selects a shape from one box. One member is blindfolded and draws a shape from the matching shape box. The member must then find the group member with the matching shape.

PARTICIPATION
PROCEDURE: The BLIND SELECTION METHOD is used to select group members. The matching member then becomes the next member to be blindfolded.

TITLE: "Stare Down"

SOCIALIZATION
GOAL AREA: Interpersonal Distance

MATERIALS: No special materials are required

GAME PROCEDURE: Two group members sit facing one another. Both members are instructed to "stare" at the other member and to keep from "cracking up"—that is, keep from laughing. The member who refrains from laughing (who stares the longest) wins the round. This member is then challenged by another member.

PARTICIPATION
PROCEDURE: For the first round, two members are chosen by the BLIND SELECTION METHOD. Thereafter, one member is chosen through the BLIND SELECTION METHOD to challenge the winner of each round.

TITLE: "Trading T-Shirts"

SOCIALIZATION
GOAL AREA: Interpersonal Distance

MATERIALS: 2 large pull-over T-shirts, kitchen timer, edible

GAME PROCEDURE: Two members sit facing each other in the center of the group. Both are given T-shirts and instructed to "put the shirt on your partner." If both shirts are on before the bell rings, each member receives a reward.

PARTICIPATION
PROCEDURE: The BLIND SELECTION METHOD is used until all members have had a turn.

TITLE: "Where's the Button?"

SOCIALIZATION
GOAL AREA: Interpersonal Distance

MATERIALS: 1 paper "button" (a circle approximately

1/2" in diameter) with adhesive tape on
the back, blindfold

GAME PROCEDURE: Group members are shown the "button"
and told that they will each have a turn
to hide the button on another group
member. One member is blindfolded and
another member hides the button. Members are encouraged to find a different
place to hide it each time. The blindfold
is removed and the individual is instructed to look for the button. The
leader is encouraged to get peer assistance or prompt systematic looking if the
member seems to be having difficulty
locating the button. One method is to
walk the member around the group
asking him or her to stop at each
member and look from the head to the
feet, both front and back.

PARTICIPATION
PROCEDURE: Pick first member through the BLIND
SELECTION METHOD. Then, the
member who finds the button becomes
the next one to hide it until all members
have had a turn.

TITLE: "Which Hand?"

SOCIALIZATION
GOAL AREA: Interpersonal Distance

MATERIALS: Bag of M & M's or other small edible

GAME PROCEDURE: A group member conceals a single M &
M in one hand and makes fists with both
hands. He/she then walks around the
inside of the circle and stops before another group member. The second member

then tries to guess which hand has the M & M. If this member is wrong then the target group member continues around the circle and stops before another member. If the member is correct, then he/she gets the M & M and assumes the role of the presentor.

PARTICIPATION
PROCEDURE: The first member is chosen through the BLIND SELECTION METHOD.

TITLE: "Working Together to Beat the Clock"

SOCIALIZATION
GOAL AREA: Interpersonal Distance

MATERIALS: Kitchen timer, ring-toss set-up, donut-shaped posterboard cut-outs, edible

GAME PROCEDURE: A donut-shaped cut-out is passed out to each group member. The group is told that the ring-toss stand will be passed around and everyone must get their cut-out on the stand and pass it to the next person.
Group members are also told that a kitchen timer will be set. If all group members get their cut-out on the stand before the timer rings then the group gets an edible reward.

PARTICIPATION
PROCEDURE: All group members are able to participate at once.

SUGGESTIONS: This game will probably take a number of practice sessions so the leader should allow time for several rounds.

KNOWING ABOUT YOURSELF

"Are You Happy or Are You Mad?"
"Feelings About Our Group"
"Finish the Sentence"
"Here's How I'm Feeling Today"
"Honk if You Know" I
"I Feel Really Good About ..."
"My Favorite Things"
"Name Warm-Up"
"Stand Up If You Agree"
"The Feeling Meter"
"Things We Like To Do Together"

TITLE: "Are You Happy or Are You Mad?"

SOCIALIZATION
GOAL AREA: Knowing About Yourself

MATERIALS: One 4" x 6" index card with a smile face drawn on it for each group member; one 4" x 6" index card with a frown face drawn on it for each group member; edible, e.g., pretzel; one "I don't care card."

GAME PROCEDURE: Members are each given two cards: one with a smile face on it and another with a frown face. Group members are told that they will be given a situation; each member must hold up the card that indicates the appropriate feeling for the situation. Group members holding up the correct card earn an edible reward. The situations provided by the group leader should be concrete. Some suggestions follow:

1. When I get to go shopping I feel _____.

2. When someone steals something of mine I feel_____.

3. When I get a letter in the mail I feel_____.

4. When I get a telephone call I feel _____.

5. When someone hits me I feel _____.

6. When someone helps me clean my room I feel _____.

7. When I make a new friend I feel _____.

8. When someone asks me to go out for a walk I feel _____.

9. When I get my paycheck at work I feel _____.

10. When my instructor tells me I'm doing a good job I feel _____.

PARTICIPATION
PROCEDURE: Everyone in the group has a chance to participate at the same time.

SUGGESTIONS: The leader may want to do about ten ˙ rounds. Concrete situations can be changed to fit in with group member's interests and preferences.

TITLE: "Feelings About Our Group"

SOCIALIZATION
GOAL AREA: Knowing About Yourself

MATERIALS: A "feeling meter" is constructed from construction paper with a pointer in the center. The meter is divided into three sections, pictorialized as happy, mad, and sad.

GAME PROCEDURE: This game is used during the termination phase of the group. A group member is presented with a structured "feeling" question and the person indicates his/her response on the "feeling meter." A member who wants to explain, discuss

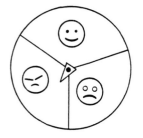

or elaborate on his/her feelings should have an opportunity to do so.
Structured questions that leaders can use include the following:
"Do you feel happy, sad or mad . . ."

1. about being in our group?"

2. about the Blindfold Game?"

3. about not having group anymore?"

4. if our group never stopped?"

5. about being a member of our group?"

6. when you think of our group?"

7. when we told you that we won't be coming here much longer?"

8. about us for saying that group can't go on?"

9. about being in another group?"

PARTICIPATION
PROCEDURE: The BLIND SELECTION METHOD is used until all members have had a turn.

SUGGESTIONS: In order to end the game positively, the leader should order questions to conclude with happy responses.

TITLE: "Finish the Sentence"

SOCIALIZATION
GOAL AREA: Knowing About Yourself

MATERIALS: No special materials are required

GAME PROCEDURE: The leader has a list of unfinished sentences. The leader explains to the group that he/she is going to present an unfinished sentence to a group member who is then supposed to finish it. The leader then moves quickly around the group giving each member a chance to finish a different sentence.

Examples of unfinished sentences follow:

1. On my hamburger I like . . .
2. For dessert I like . . .
3. My favorite TV show is . . .
4. My chore is . . .
5. When I need help with a problem I can go to . . .
6. When it's snack time I like to drink . . .
7. My favorite color is . . ./I like pictures of . . .
8. When I have free time I like to . . .
9. On my hot dog I like . . .
10. My Christmas wish is to . . .

PARTICIPATION
PROCEDURE: The LEADER SELECTION METHOD is used by moving around the group giving each member a turn.

TITLE: "Here's How I'm Feeling Today"

SOCIALIZATION
GOAL AREA: Knowing About Yourself

MATERIALS: 3 cards depicting happy, mad, and sad faces

GAME PROCEDURE: A member draws one of the cards from the set and is instructed to act out the feeling without telling the group what it is. The leader asks the members to raise their hands if they know the feeling. The member identifying the feeling becomes the next participant.

PARTICIPATION
PROCEDURE: The LEADER SELECTION METHOD

is used until all members have had a turn.

SUGGESTIONS: The leader may introduce the cards by passing them around the group to get members to identify the feelings represented by the cards. The leaders may also model each feeling prior prior to playing the game.

TITLE: "Honk If You Know" I

SOCIALIZATION
GOAL AREA: Knowing About Yourself

MATERIALS: Bicycle horn

GAME PROCEDURE: The leader shows horn to group and demonstrates noise it makes. Members are told that the leader will ask a question and if group members know an answer they can come up (one at a time) to honk horn and give answer.
Possible questions include:

1. What is your favorite thing to eat?

2. Who is your favorite friend?

3. What is your favorite activity?

4. What is your favorite T.V. show?

5. Where is your favorite place to go? (at home or in town)

6. What is your favorite color?

7. What color is your favorite shirt?

PARTICIPATION
PROCEDURE: Each member should be encouraged to come before group, honk the horn, and answer a question. The LEADER SELECTION METHOD is used.

SUGGESTIONS: Questions can be added to fit in with

the group member's interests, preferences and activities.

TITLE: "I Feel Really Good About . . ."

SOCIALIZATION
GOAL AREA: Knowing About Yourself

MATERIALS: No special materials are required

GAME PROCEDURE: A group member is seated in the center of the circle. The leader presents him/her with a situation to which he/she must state whether he/she would feel good or bad about the specific situation. After the chosen member responds, group members then have an opportunity to express their feelings about the specific situation. This can be done through a group vote, e.g., leader asks "Who else feels good about this situation?" or "Who feels bad about this situation?" The group member can be helped to count the number of group members who feel like him/her.

Suggested situations are:
"Do you feel good or bad when . . .
You are wearing your favorite outfit."
You get to go on a trip."
You get in a fight with your best friend."
Your instructor tells you that you did a good job."
Your clothes are torn."
Your friend invites you over to his/her house for dinner."
Someone teases you."
You lose your paycheck."
You get to go to a baseball game."
You lose your wallet (or handbag)."
You help your friend go shopping."

You have enough money to buy new clothes."
You sleep late and you are late for work."
You have enough money to take a friend to a movie."
You go to a party."
Your friend is sick."

PARTICIPATION
PROCEDURE: The BLIND SELECTION METHOD is used.

SUGGESTIONS: The leader may want to introduce the concept of "feeling good" or "feeling bad" about oneself by suggesting that there are things that can make us feel good about ourselves. Some of these things are: (1) helping others; (2) sharing with others; (3) looking clean and neat, etc. Also, leader suggests that there are things that can make us feel bad such as: (1) arguing with friends; (2) not being able to go places we want; (3) not having enough money.

TITLE: "My Favorite Things"

SOCIALIZATION
GOAL AREA: Knowing About Yourself

MATERIALS: Kitchen timer with bell

GAME PROCEDURE: Members are presented with a concrete category, e.g., food, and are asked to come up with something that they like within that category. The leader sets the kitchen timer and moves around the circle asking each group member to say something different within the assigned category. When the bell of the timer rings then the leader changes to a new category. Examples of categories are:

1. Food
2. Friends
3. Favorite thing to do during spare time
4. Wish for Christmas
5. Season of the year
6. T.V. show
7. Favorite spot in residence
8. Favorite spot in the community
9. Snack

PARTICIPATION
PROCEDURE: The LEADER SELECTION METHOD is used by moving around the group in order, giving each member a turn.

SUGGESTIONS: Categories can be changed to fit in with group member's interests and preferences.

TITLE: "Name Warm-Up"

SOCIALIZATION
GOAL AREA: Knowing About Yourself

MATERIALS: Standard set of pictures

GAME PROCEDURE: Each member selects his/her picture from the group and shows it to other group members. He/she is instructed to introduce himself/herself, i.e. "My name is _____" and tell about something he/she likes to do, knows how to do or wants to learn.

PARTICIPATION
PROCEDURE: The BLIND SELECTION METHOD is used.

TITLE: "Stand Up If You Agree"

SOCIALIZATION
GOAL AREA: Knowing About Yourself

MATERIALS: No special materials are required

GAME PROCEDURE: Members are verbally presented with a concrete activity, food or situation and they must decide whether they like it or not. If the member likes or enjoys doing the activity then he/she stands up after the leader's cue.

The leader starts the game by saying: "We are going to say some things that you all may like or may not like to do. If you like to do the thing we say then you should stand up."

The leader's cue will be "Stand up if you like . . .". Some examples:

"Stand up if you : . .

1. like to eat spinach."

2. like to go swimming."

3. like to be teased."

4. like to eat pizza."

5. like to sleep late on Saturdays."

6. like to go to have lunch with a friend."

7. like to go to bed early."

8. like to get into fights."

9. like to have a good friend."

10. like to be yelled at."

11. like to take a walk with someone."

12. like to share a secret with a friend."

13. like to have a date."

PARTICIPATION
PROCEDURE: Everyone in the group has a chance to participate at the same time.

SUGGESTIONS: The leader may want to do about ten rounds. Also, the leader may want to develop his/her own concrete examples to personalize the game for group members.

TITLE: "The Feeling Meter"

SOCIALIZATION
GOAL AREA: Knowing About Yourself

MATERIALS: A feeling meter is constructed from construction paper, with a pointer in the center. The meter is divided into three sections, pictorialized as happy, mad, and sad.

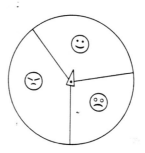

GAME PROCEDURE: The member draws a situation from the "Feeling Box" and then is instructed to go to the "Feeling Meter" and point the arrow to the feeling that matches the situation. Suggestions for situations are listed in "Are You Happy or Are You Mad?" (page 66).

PARTICIPATION
PROCEDURE: The BLIND SELECTION METHOD is used until all members have had a turn.

TITLE: "Things We Like To Do Together"

SOCIALIZATION
GOAL AREA: Knowing About Yourself

MATERIALS: Pictures of other activities members could do in a group, i.e., eat, swim, picnic, take walks, dance, go to movies

GAME PROCEDURE: Leader asks members to verbalize what they did in their group; i.e. play games. Leader asks members to think about other activities the group could do together. Each member is asked to select from the activity box one of the activity pictures. Members are asked to vote with raised hands indicating whether they like to do each activity with someone.

PARTICIPATION
PROCEDURE: The BLIND SELECTION METHOD is used.

KNOWING ABOUT OTHERS

"Back-to-Back"

"Can You Pretend?"

"Clothing Color Match"

"Find the Owner"

"Find Your Friend"

"Find the Person"

"Honk If You Know" II

"I Know Something About You"

"If I Were a Staff Member"

"Name Draw"

"Name Game" I

"Name Game" II

"Pick a Friend"

"Put on the Thinkin' Cap"

"The Blindfold Game"

"TV Star"

"We Had a Great Group!"

"We Have A Lot in Common"

"Whisper"

"Who Am I Talking About?"

"Who Is This Person?"

"Who's Missing?"

"Who's Talking?"

TITLE: "Back-to-Back"

SOCIALIZATION
GOAL AREA: Knowing About Others

MATERIALS: No special materials are required

GAME PROCEDURE: The object of the game is "to think about what our partners in the game like and to tell this to the group." Two members then sit back-to-back in the center of the group and grasp hands. The first member selected must tell the group something that his/her partner likes. If he/she is correct the partner releases one hand. The active participant must then tell something different that the partner likes in order to have his/her other hand released. Roles are then reversed.

PARTICIPATION
PROCEDURE: The BLIND SELECTION METHOD is used to select two members at a time until all members have had a turn.

TITLE: "Can You Pretend?"

SOCIALIZATION
GOAL AREA: Knowing About Others

MATERIALS: No special materials are required

GAME PROCEDURE: A group member is selected to draw a name of another group member from a box. The leader then whispers the name of this group member to the selected member and tells him/her to make believe he/she is this person. The goal is to get the selected group member to imitate another group member. The group then tries to guess who is being imitated by the selected member.

Once the group member who is being
imitated is identified he/she gets the
next turn.

PARTICIPATION
PROCEDURE: The first member is selected through the
BLIND SELECTION METHOD. After
this, group members who are imitated
and identified by the group get a turn.

TITLE: "Clothing Color Match"

SOCIALIZATION
GOAL AREA: Knowing About Others

MATERIALS: Ten index cards; each card has one of the
following colors on it: black, blue,
red, brown, yellow, green, orange, pink,
gold, white. (Note: colors can be put
on cards with crayons).

GAME PROCEDURE: Index cards are placed in a box. A group
member selects a card from the box
and identifies the color. The member
then walks around group and attempts
to find another member who is wearing some piece of clothing that contains
the chosen color.

PARTICIPATION
PROCEDURE: The BLIND SELECTION METHOD is
used to select the initial person. Thereafter, the person who is identified as
wearing the selected color gets the opportunity to draw a card from the box.

SUGGESTIONS: The leader may want to bring a box of
crayons and a small supply of index cards
into the group. The leader should scan
the group to see what colors are being
worn. The leader can then make up some

additional cards if necessary. By scanning beforehand, the leader will insure that each member will be chosen.

TITLE: "Find the Owner"

SOCIALIZATION
GOAL AREA: Knowing About Others

MATERIALS: Box containing objects belonging to group members, e.g., watch, necklace, ring, cup, key, barrette, book, etc., blindfold.

GAME PROCEDURE: Members are asked to donate one of their personal possessions to the group box. A member is then blindfolded. The blindfolded member must return it to its proper owner.

PARTICIPATION
PROCEDURE: The BLIND SELECTION METHOD is used until all members have had a turn.

TITLE: "Find Your Friend"

SOCIALIZATION
GOAL AREA: Knowing About Others

MATERIALS: Blindfold, standard pictures (see p. 40)

GAME PROCEDURE: One member is blindfolded. Another member selects a picture from all pictures with faces down and leads the blind-folded member around the circle to locate this member. The pair is instructed to stop at each member who in turn is to say "Hi." The leading member then inquires "Is this Sue?" and continues around the group until the individual is identified.

PARTICIPATION
PROCEDURE: The BLIND SELECTION METHOD is used, with the leading member and the member identified becoming the next pair.

TITLE: "Find the Person"

SOCIALIZATION
GOAL AREA: Knowing About Others

MATERIALS: Twenty index cards are needed. These cards are divided up into two piles of ten cards each. One pile of cards represent personal objects. A picture is sketched on each card with pencil or crayon. These pictures can include: (1) glasses; (2) pocketbook; (3) dress; (4) slacks; (5) earrings; (6) ring/jewelry; (7) socks; (8) tennis shoes; (9) hat; and (10) shorts. Another set of cards, personal characteristics, can contain pictures of the following: (1) a face with freckles; (2) a person with short hair; (3) a person with long hair; (4) a face with a smile; (5) a person wearing braided hair; (6) a short person standing next to a tall person; (7) a person with blonde hair; (8) a person with brown hair; (9) a skinny person; and (10) a person with straight hair.

GAME PROCEDURE: The set of "personal object" cards are placed in a box. A group member selects a card from the box, and identifies the object. The member then walks around the group and locates another member who has the selected object. After the personal object cards are used, then the "personal characteristic" cards are placed in the box.

PARTICIPATION
PROCEDURE: The BLIND SELECTION METHOD
is used to select the initial person. Thereafter the person who is identified as
having the selected object or characteris-
- tic gets the opportunity to draw a card
from the box.

SUGGESTIONS: This game requires that the leaders know
group members fairly well. The per-
sonal objects and characteristics listed
above were designed for a group whose
membership was women. Other leaders
may feel that these are not appropriate
for a particular group, so other objects
and characteristics can be developed.
For instance, for a group of men, the
following could be used: (1) a person with
a moustache; (2) a person with a beard;
(3) a person smoking a pipe. The important point is that the leader should
get members to observe the personal
characteristics of other people.

TITLE: "Honk If You Know" II
SOCIALIZATION
GOAL AREA: Knowing About Others
MATERIALS: Bicycle horn
GAME PROCEDURE: The leader starts off game by honking
the horn and saying, "I know something
about (Sally)! She (likes to go to the store),
(doesn't like coffee), (wants to go to
the zoo), (has a new sweater), (etc.). The
leader then opens up the game to the
group by saying, "If anyone else can tell
us something about (Sally) you can raise
your hand, come up, blow the horn and
tell us."

One round of this game is complete after everyone who raises their hand has had a chance to blow the horn and say something about the target person.

PARTICIPATION
PROCEDURE: The target member is chosen by the BLIND SELECTION METHOD. However, in order to get a turn to honk the horn, the leader requires group members to raise their hands.

TITLE: "I Know Something About You"

SOCIALIZATION
GOAL AREA: Knowing About Others

MATERIALS: Blindfold, edible (pretzel)

GAME PROCEDURE: Two members are seated in the center of the circle and given 1 minute to look at each other. Following the minute they are blindfolded one at a time and asked questions about each other. Each right answer is rewarded with a pretzel. Sample questions are:
What color is your partner's hair?
Does he/she have glasses on?
Does he/she have a dress or pants on?
Does he/she have shoes on?
Does he/she have on the color red?

PARTICIPATION
PROCEDURE: The BLIND SELECTION METHOD is used picking two members at a time.

TITLE: "If I Were a Staff Member"

SOCIALIZATION
GOAL AREA: Knowing About Others

MATERIALS: No special materials required

GAME PROCEDURE: A member is selected and asked by the leader to tell or show the group members something that staff members do on the ward. Each member must contribute something different with prompting from the group permissible.

To decrease the difficulty level of the game it is suggested that the facilitators provide categories of activities, i.e. things to keep the ward looking nice, things to help the residents on or off the ward.

PARTICIPATION
PROCEDURE: The BLIND SELECTION METHOD is recommended with each member in turn selecting the next participant.

TITLE: "Name Draw"

SOCIALIZATION
GOAL AREA: Knowing About Others

MATERIALS: Standard set of pictures

GAME PROCEDURE: The leader presents all pictures face down in a card hand fashion to one member. The member is instructed to draw a picture and take it to the proper person saying, "I'm _____, what is your name?" After being told the name, he/she gives them the picture and introduces the member to the group. ("This is _____.) The member introduced then follows the same procedure.

PARTICIPATION
PROCEDURE: The BLIND SELECTION METHOD is used.

SUGGESTIONS: For an advanced version, the second person adds a second picture, introducing himself/herself, the first picture, and

asking the name of the person's picture
he/she draws. Each member continues to
add pictures with the final member introducing all pictures of the group.

TITLE: "Name Game" I

SOCIALIZATION
GOAL AREA: Knowing About Others

MATERIALS: Rolled up socks

GAME PROCEDURE: Each member is instructed to call out the
name of someone in the group before
tossing the socks to them. The game proceeds with members catching the socks
and then throwing them to another
member.

PARTICIPATION
PROCEDURE: Starting member is selected by BLIND
SELECTION METHOD.

TITLE: "Name Game" II

SOCIALIZATION
GOAL AREA: Knowing About Others

MATERIALS: Rolled up socks, standard pictures

GAME PROCEDURE: One member is selected as a name
caller and calls members' names one at
a time by pulling from pictures. As
he/she calls the name, the person with
the socks throws them to the named
individual. The caller continues until the
timer rings. The timer should be set
for from 3-5 minutes to permit each
member to be a caller.

PARTICIPATION
PROCEDURE: The BLIND SELECTION METHOD
is used.

TITLE: "Pick A Friend"

SOCIALIZATION
GOAL AREA: Knowing About Others

MATERIALS: M & M's

GAME PROCEDURE: A group member is selected and seated within the circle. The selected member holds out both hands, palms up, and one M & M is placed in each one. The selected member is instructed to look around the group at each member's clothing. He/she is told to select a person but not say his/her name. The selected member gives a clue about the person by saying something about the color of his/her clothing. For example, the seated member says: "I am thinking of someone wearing blue shoes." Everyone tries to identify the person. When correctly identified, the person comes up and takes an M & M from the member's hand, and the seated member gets the other M & M.

PARTICIPATION
PROCEDURE: The BLIND SELECTION METHOD is used to select one group member at a time.

TITLE: "Put on the Thinkin' Cap"

SOCIALIZATION
GOAL AREA: Knowing About Others

MATERIALS: A hat (appropriate to group members)

GAME PROCEDURE: The leader shows the group the "Thinkin' Cap" and says, "When we wear this hat it helps us think about what other people like to do, or something that makes them happy."
Two members sit in the middle of the

group facing each other. One member puts on the "Thinkin' Cap" and is asked to think of or do something to make his/her partner happy, e.g., say something friendly, share a belonging. If correct, the roles are reversed and the partner must put on the "Thinkin' Cap." If incorrect, the member is asked to try again.

PARTICIPATION
PROCEDURE: The BLIND SELECTION METHOD is used to select two members at a time until all have had a turn.

SUGGESTIONS: For members having difficulty with this task, other group members may be asked to assist.

TITLE: "The Blindfold Game"

SOCIALIZATION
GOAL AREA: Knowing About Others

MATERIALS: Blindfold

GAME PROCEDURE: One group member is seated before the group and is blindfolded. Another member is selected to sit beside the blindfolded person. The leader then guides the blindfolded person in touching the other person's hair, nose, eyes, mouth. After touching these features the blindfolded person is asked to guess the identity of the person who is seated next to him/her. If the blindfolded person does not have sufficient information, the other person can give an auditory cue by saying "Hi." The blindfolded person is then given another chance to guess.

PARTICIPATION
PROCEDURE: The blindfolded member is selected

through the BLIND SELECTION
METHOD. The other member is selected
by the LEADER SELECTION
METHOD.

SUGGESTIONS: A basic procedure that the leader can
use to instruct blindfolded members
can involve the following questions:
(1) Touch the member's hair. Is it smooth
or curly? Is it long or short? (2) Touch
the person's nose. Is it big or small?
(3) Touch the person's skin. Is it rough
or smooth? (4) Can you guess who this
person is?

TITLE: "TV Star"

SOCIALIZATION
GOAL AREA: Knowing About Others

MATERIALS: Standard photographs of each group
member, a television screen drawn on a
cardboard with slits so that a photograph
can be placed in the screen, edible

GAME PROCEDURE: A group member's photograph is selected
from a box of photos. The person is
identified by another group member and
it is announced that this is "The (Sally
Wilson) television show." The leader
then places the photograph in the television screen. The "TV Star" is asked
to come before group and is given a bag
of edibles, e.g., pretzels. The group
is then asked, "What do you like about
this person?". If a group member contributes a positive comment then the
"TV Star" rewards the contributor with
an edible.

PARTICIPATION
PROCEDURE: The BLIND SELECTION METHOD is used to select the "TV Star."

SUGGESTIONS: This game depends on the leader playing up the idea that the group members will be "TV Stars." It is beneficial if the leader plays up a group member having his/her own television show and the leader should work at making the selected person the center of attention.

TITLE: "We Had a Great Group!"

SOCIALIZATION
GOAL AREA: Knowing About Others

MATERIALS: Group pictures for all members

GAME PROCEDURE: The leader holds up the group picture and presents a riddle about each member telling members for example, "This good group member likes (to sing)," etc. The member who guesses the identity takes a group picture from the leader and presents it to the member. Members are encouraged to clap for each person "who was a really good group member." The procedure continues until all have received a group picture.

PARTICIPATION
PROCEDURE: LEADER SELECTION METHOD is used.

TITLE: "We Have A Lot In Common"

SOCIALIZATION
GOAL AREA: Knowing About Others

MATERIALS: No special materials are required

GAME PROCEDURE: The leader explains to group members that there are many ways that we are alike and many ways that we are different. Two stations or areas are set up on opposite sides of the members' circle. The leader then tells the members that "We are going to find out how we are alike and how we are different." The leader presents members with forced-choice characteristics. If the members have the characteristic, they are instructed to go to one of the stations. If not, they go to the other. The leader then draws attention to the fact that, "This is a way in which some of us are different," or "this is a way in which we are all alike."

The following characteristics could be used in this game:

1. Sex

2. Hair color

3. Height — tall or short

4. Size — big or little

5. Wears glasses or doesn't wear glasses

6. Likes school or doesn't like school

7. Likes specific types of food

8. Favorite color

PARTICIPATION
PROCEDURE: All group members participate simultaneously.

SUGGESTIONS: Questions can be added to fit in with the group member's interests, preferences and activities.

TITLE: "Whisper"

SOCIALIZATION
GOAL AREA: Knowing About Others

MATERIALS: Blindfold

GAME PROCEDURE: A group member is blindfolded and placed in the middle of the group. Another member is selected to go up to the blindfolded member and whisper something in his/her ear. The "whispering" member then returns to his/her seat. The blindfold is removed and the member is asked to point to the one who he/she thinks whispered to him/her. If the member is correct, the game proceeds until all members have had a turn. If the member is wrong, the original blindfold process is repeated.

PARTICIPATION
PROCEDURE: The BLIND SELECTION METHOD is used.

SUGGESTIONS: To encourage involvement, the group may be encouraged to say "yes" or "no" after the blindfolded member makes his/her choice.

TITLE: "Who Am I Talking About?"

SOCIALIZATION
GOAL AREA: Knowing About Others

MATERIALS: Full length photo of each member.

GAME PROCEDURE: A group member is seated in the center of the group and asked to select one photo from the group of photos. The member is instructed to look at the photo so that he/she can answer some questions about the person pictured.

The following questions may be used:

1. Is this person a man or woman?
2. Is this person tall or short?
3. Does this person have long or short hair?
4. Does this person wear glasses?
5. Does this person have a beard or moustache (if applicable)?
6. Does this person have curly or straight hair?
7. What is this person wearing?

After each question, the leader asks the rest of the group to guess the identity of the person described; and to raise their hands if they know. Whoever correctly guesses goes into the center of the group for his/her turn.

PARTICIPATION
PROCEDURE: The LEADER SELECTION METHOD is used until all members have had a turn.

TITLE: "Who Is This Person"

SOCIALIZATION
GOAL AREA: Knowledge About Others

MATERIALS: Standard set of pictures

GAME PROCEDURE: The leader passes a photograph around the circle, of which the head is not visible (covered with paper). Each group member is asked to look at the photograph and try to think who the person is without telling the group. The leader than walks around the circle touching different members on the head and asking the group to raise their hands if the "mystery person" is being touched. When the "mystery person" is correctly identified, he/she is asked to come into the center of the group to display his/her picture.

PARTICIPATION
PROCEDURE: The leader uses the BLIND SELECTION METHOD, drawing one picture at a time from the group of pictures placed face down. The game continues until all members have had a turn as the "mystery person."

TITLE: "Who's Missing . . ."

SOCIALIZATION
GOAL AREA: Knowing About Others

MATERIALS: No special materials are required

GAME PROCEDURE: Group members are instructed to close their eyes. The leader explains that he/she will tap someone on the shoulder and then lead that person away from the group. Group members are then told to open their eyes and look around the group to try to guess "who's missing."

PARTICIPATION
PROCEDURE: The LEADER SELECTION METHOD is used until all members have had a turn.

SUGGESTIONS: Leadership can rotate among those members who are interested.

TITLE: "Who's Talking?"

SOCIALIZATION
GOAL AREA: Knowing About Others

MATERIALS: A tape recorder is used to record the

voices of all group members at a session other than when the game is introduced. Members are asked to tell something about themselves without saying their names.

GAME PROCEDURE: One group member sits in the middle of the group. The leader plays a voice and instructs the seated member to listen very carefully to the voice to figure out "Who's Talking?". If the member is unable to identify the voice, it should be repeated. If he/she is still unable to identify the voice, another group member should be selected to come up and whisper the name of the mystery voice to the seated member.

PARTICIPATION
PROCEDURE: The BLIND SELECTION METHOD is used until all members have had a turn.

PROSOCIAL

"Friendship Chain"
"Helping Each Other"
"Helping My Friend Find His/Her Stuff"
"Helping My Neighbor" I
"Helping My Neighbor" II
"I Have a Problem. How Can You Help?"
"The Magic Box" I
"The Magic Box" II

TITLE: "Friendship Chain"

SOCIALIZATION
GOAL AREA: Prosocial

MATERIALS: Piece of string approximately 3 feet long for each member.

GAME PROCEDURE: A member stands in the middle of the circle and is asked to tell the group something he/she could do for a friend. The group is instructed to vote "weird" or "OK." If "OK" the individual is given the first string or link of the "Friendship Chain." If "weird" the individual is asked to try again. Another member then comes into the center of the circle and must tell the group something different that he/she would do for a friend. If correct, he/she is given his/her string and it is tied to the string of the original member.

PARTICIPATION
PROCEDURE: The BLIND SELECTION METHOD is used until all members are tied onto the "Friendship Chain."

TITLE: "Helping Each Other"

SOCIALIZATION
GOAL AREA: Prosocial

MATERIALS: Pairs of objects that may be used together are separated into two boxes, e.g., necklace and bracelet, comb and brush, crayon and paper, toothbrush and toothpaste, soap and towel, cup and pop can; matched clothing may be used.

GAME PROCEDURE: One member is blindfolded. All other members select an item from one box.

The blindfolded member selects an item from the match box. The blindfold is removed and the member must then locate the individual who has an item that can be used with or complements the selected item.

PARTICIPATION
PROCEDURE: The BLIND SELECTION METHOD is used with the matching member becoming the next to be blindfolded.

TITLE: "Helping My Friend Find His/Her Stuff"

SOCIALIZATION
GOAL AREA: Prosocial

MATERIALS: Various small articles that may be hidden, e.g., cup, book, purse—may be the personal articles of group members

GAME PROCEDURE: One group member is escorted away from the group, preferably out of the room, but may stand with back towards group. A second group member is instructed to hide an article. The removed member is brought back to the group and instructed to find his/her missing article. The group is instructed to assist by saying "warmer" as the member approaches the hidden article, or "colder" if the member moves away from the article. After the article is located, the game proceeds until all members have had a turn.

PARTICIPATION
PROCEDURE: The BLIND SELECTION METHOD is used.

SUGGESTIONS: The leader may request that the searching member pause at regular intervals at which time the group is asked and prompted if necessary to indicate "warmer" or "colder."

TITLE: "Helping My Neighbor" I

SOCIALIZATION
GOAL AREA: Prosocial

MATERIALS: Examples are: umbrella, hairbrush, pullover hat, gloves, wash cloth, sun glasses, hand lotion, rubber boots, magazine

GAME PROCEDURE: Group members are told that this is a game to discover how we can help our friends. A group member comes up and sits before the group. Materials are laid out on the table. The leader then says "Her name is (Cindy), she's stuck out in the rain. Can anyone discover a way to help her?" The leader then selects a member who raises his/her hand to come up and solve the problem for the target group member.
The leader continues this strategy with different members sitting before the group. Questions asked of the group can involve:

1. staying warm

2. keeping one's hair neat

3. staying clean

4. keeping the sun out of one's eyes

5. keeping one's feet dry

6. needing something to do, e.g., look at magazine.

7. keeping one's hands smooth

PARTICIPATION
PROCEDURE: The BLIND SELECTION METHOD
is used.

SUGGESTIONS: This game can be personalized for group members in order to promote their interpersonal problem solving.

TITLE: "Helping My Neighbor" II

SOCIALIZATION
GOAL AREA: Prosocial

MATERIALS: No special materials are required

GAME PROCEDURE: A group member is seated before the group. The leader provides a hypothetical situation: "Here's (Cindy). She can't find anything to do and she is bored. Can anyone find her something to do?" A group member is then selected to help the target member.

Hypothetical situations the leader can use include:

1. "Here's _____. She's really angry. What can someone do to make her feel better?"

2. "Here's _____. She's having a seizure. How can we help?"

3. "Here's _____. She's feeling sad. What can someone do to make her feel better?"

4. "Here's _____. She has cut her finger. How can someone help her?"

5. "Here's _____. She is really cold. Who can help her?"

6. "Here's _____. She's sick to her stomach. Who can help her?"

7. "Here's _____. She tells you that she's very thirsty. Who can help her?"

PARTICIPATION
PROCEDURE: One group member is selected each time through the BLIND SELECTION METHOD.

TITLE: "I Have a Problem. How Can You Help?"

SOCIALIZATION
GOAL AREA: Prosocial

MATERIALS: No special materials are required

GAME PROCEDURE: A group member is given a problem by the leader. Another group member is selected to solve the problem and together they work toward a solution. Roles are then reversed using a different problem.
Possible problem situations:

1. Needs to brush his/her hair but can't find a brush.
2. Can't zip a back zipper.
3. Needs a cup for coffee.
4. Hurt his/her hand and can't make the bed without help.
5. Is sick in bed and would like some water.
6. Needs to move something heavy.
7. Fell down and is hurt.
8. Wants to be alone.
9. Wants to play a game.
10. Lost his/her wallet/purse.
11. Is feeling lonely.

PARTICIPATION
PROCEDURE: The BLIND SELECTION METHOD
is recommended, selecting two individuals at a time.

TITLE: "The Magic Box" I

SOCIALIZATION
GOAL AREA: Prosocial

MATERIALS: Standard photographs of each group
member, box with small wrapped candies
or pennies

GAME PROCEDURE: Before the game is introduced, the leader
tapes two candies or pennies to the back
of each picture. The leader explains that
he/she is going to pass around a "Magic
Box." A member selects a picture, identifies the person, and then shares the
prize with the person.

PARTICIPATION
PROCEDURE: The BLIND SELECTION METHOD is
used until all members have had a
turn.

TITLE: "The Magic Box" II

SOCIALIZATION
GOAL AREA: Prosocial

MATERIALS: Standard photographs of each group
member, attached stick figure pictures
depicting two members holding hands,
combing hair, patting backs, etc.

GAME PROCEDURE: Before the start of the session, the
leader tapes one of the activities to the
back of each picture. The leader explains
that he/she is going to pass the "Magic

Box" to one member. The member is instructed to draw a picture and then complete the activity with that individual.

PARTICIPATION
PROCEDURE: The BLIND SELECTION METHOD is used with each person drawn in turn drawing the next participant.

SUGGESTIONS: Sample suggested drawings are:

| Waving | Shaking hands | Holding both hands | Arms around each other | Standing back to back | Hooking arms |

SOCIAL COMPETENCE

"Being Responsible" I
"Being Responsible" II
"Don't Lose Your Cool" I
"Don't Lose Your Cool" II
"Mix and Match"
"Planning for Comfort"
"Should I Ask for Help?"
"Something's Wrong with Those Clothes!"
"The Greeting Game"
"What Am I Doing?"
"What Am I Dressed For?"
"Who Can Help?"

TITLE: "Being Responsible" I

SOCIALIZATION
GOAL AREA: Social competence

MATERIALS: Index cards for each member with a picture of an adult-looking person and the word "responsible"

GAME PROCEDURE: Each member is given one of the stimulus cards. The leader then presents one situation at a time (enacts and/or verbalizes) to which members must decide whether the behavior was responsible or not. If the situation represents responsible behavior, members are instructed to hold up their cards. If not, the card remains in their laps.
Possible situations include:

1. Individual doesn't do his chores.

2. Individual is tired and trades chores with someone else.

3. Individual is sick and doesn't go to work.

4. Individual is sick and calls work to tell them he won't be in.

5. Individual is sick but doesn't want to tell anyone.

6. Individual is sick and tells a staff person or goes to the doctor.

7. Individual wants to use a friend's shampoo so he takes it.

8. Individual asks to borrow a friend's shampoo.

9. Individual is upset with a friend so he hits him.

10. Individual is upset with a friend and talks to him about it.

11. Individual goes to work when he feels like it.

12. Individual goes to work every day.

PARTICIPATION
PROCEDURE: All members participate at the same time.

TITLE: "Being Responsible" II

SOCIALIZATION
GOAL AREA: Social competence

MATERIALS: Small box or container, slips of paper listing each problem situation

GAME PROCEDURE: One member selects a problem slip from the container. The problem is read to the group. The member is asked to solve the problem in a responsible way. Other group members are encouraged to provide other ways of solving the problem.

PARTICIPATION
PROCEDURE: The BLIND SELECTION METHOD is used.

SUGGESTIONS: Topic areas include being responsible at work, in the home, in the community, or with friends. Leaders are encouraged to make problems specific to the needs of the group.

TITLE: "Don't Lose Your Cool!" II

SOCIALIZATION
GOAL AREA: Social competence

MATERIALS: No special materials are required

GAME PROCEDURE: One member is selected to go to the center of the circle. The leader gives the member a situation, changing for each individual, and asks the member what he/she would do. The group is prompted to respond to the center member. If he/she responds in a socially appropriate way, the group responds "He/she was cool"; if not, the response is "He/she lost his/her cool!"
Situations:

1. Staff won't give you cigarettes.

2. You can't find your shirt.

3. Someone hit you for no reason.

4. You want some money.

5. You want to see the social worker right away.

6. You feel too sick to go to work.

7. You just don't want to go to work.

8. You're told by a staff member to wait for coffee.

9. A staff person says you must make your bed before you get coffee.

10. Someone gives you the finger or makes a fist.

11. Your class or work is cancelled.

12. Someone calls you a name.

13. At work, you're asked to do something you don't want to do.

TITLE: "Mix and Match"

SOCIALIZATION
GOAL AREA: Social competence

MATERIALS: Basket of pants and tops or shirts (four of each with obvious matches), edible

GAME PROCEDURE: One group member is selected to make an outfit from the basket. The group judges whether the outfit is "weird" or "OK." If the outfit is OK the member receives a pretzel. If "weird" the member draws the name of someone else to help. When the outfit is judged as "OK" both receive a pretzel.

PARTICIPATION
PROCEDURE: The BLIND SELECTION METHOD is used.

SUGGESTIONS: This game may be increased in difficulty level by requiring the member to "beat the clock" or perform task in _____ no. seconds. In addition, other clothing items, shoes, underwear, may be added to require a complete set of clothing.

TITLE: "Planning for Comfort"

SOCIALIZATION
GOAL AREA: Social competence

MATERIALS: Cards depicting weather conditions: sun and swimming, rain and umbrella, snow and snowman. Rain coat, hat, coat, sweater, boots, shorts, sandles.

GAME PROCEDURE: One member selects a weather condition from the three stimulus cards: (1) hot and sunny, (2) rain, (3) snow and cold. Another member is selected and taken away from the group by the leader to select an article of clothing. The member comes to the group and the group votes as to whether the clothing is "weird" or "OK." for the weather. If weird, a member is selected by raised hands to assist. The procedure is continued until all members have had a turn.

PARTICIPATION
PROCEDURE: The BLIND SELECTION METHOD is used.

TITLE: "Should I Ask For Help?"

SOCIALIZATION
GOAL AREA: Social competence

MATERIALS: Container with slips of paper for each situation

GAME PROCEDURE: A member selects a situation from the problem box and must decide whether he/she needs help or can solve it on his/her own. Members are asked to respond with "I need help," or "I can do it myself." For less verbal members, "yes," or "no" or headshakes indicating yes or no would be appropriate. Possible situations include:

1. You fell down but aren't hurt.

2. You fell down and hurt your leg.

3. You haven't done your chores.

4. You don't know how to do a chore.

5. You can't find your money but haven't looked.

6. Your money was stolen.

7. You need some shampoo or toothpaste.

8. The shampoo is all gone.

9. It's time to get ready for work.

10. You need some new clothes.

11. Your room (locker) is a mess.

12. Something in your room is broken and needs to be fixed.

PARTICIPATION
PROCEDURE: The BLIND SELECTION METHOD is used.

TITLE: "Something's Wrong with Those Clothes!"

SOCIALIZATION
GOAL AREA: Social competence

MATERIALS: Articles of clothing that need repair, e.g., broken zipper, missing buttons; articles that are too large; articles that don't match.

GAME PROCEDURE: A member is selected to leave the area. The leader assists the member in putting on clothing or modifying their own clothing so that it is inappropriate. The person then enters the area and group members are asked to raise their hands when they recognize the problem with the person's clothing. One member is selected to go up, and point to what is inappropriate and to help the person fix the clothing.

Examples of modifications include:

1. Wearing a slightly torn shirt.

2. Rolling up pant legs.

3. Untying shoe laces.

4. Tucking pants into socks.

5. Putting a sweater on backwards.

6. Wearing socks that don't match.

7. Wearing a shirt missing a button.

8. Wearing a shirt that is buttoned wrong.

9. Wearing a sweater that is inside out.

10. Wearing shoes on the wrong feet.

11. Having underwear sticking out.

PARTICIPATION
PROCEDURE: The BLIND SELECTION METHOD is used to select one group member at a time.

SUGGESTIONS: This game can be modified to deal with idiosyncratic dressing behavior. For instance, on one ward people may wear heavy coats or winter hats when the living environment is well heated. The leader may want to present these situations to the group so that people can get group feedback about appropriate dressing.

TITLE: "The Greeting Game"

SOCIALIZATION
GOAL AREA: Social competence

MATERIALS: No special materials are required

GAME PROCEDURE: The leader role plays a "weird" greeting, e.g., hugging a person or pulling at a person, and then role plays an "OK" greeting (e.g., shaking hands or holding up hand and saying "Hi!"). After each role play the leader asks group members whether the scene was "weird" or "OK." The leader selects two group members to role play a greeting scene. Other group members can rate the role play scene as either "weird" or "OK." In order to encourage the group members who are role playing to use "OK" behavior, each person should have a chance to role play both "weird" and "OK" ways of greeting. Suggestions for role play:

WEIRD

1. Hugging another person.
2. Kissing another person.
3. Pulling at a person.
4. Grabbing someone from behind.
5. Grabbing someone's belt.
6. Holding hands with visitor.
7. Making direct face contact with someone.

OK

1. Shaking hands.
2. Holding up hand to wave.
3. Verbal phrases:
   a. "Hi!"
   b. "What's your name?"
   c. "My name is ..."

The session should end by involving group members in "OK" role plays.

PARTICIPATION
PROCEDURE: The BLIND SELECTION PROCEDURE is used to select two group members at a time until all members have participated.

SUGGESTIONS: This game model may be used to address learning about social rules in various settings, i.e., appropriate table manners, locating restrooms, asking for help, dating, sexual activity.

TITLE: "What Am I Doing?"

SOCIALIZATION
GOAL AREA: Social competence

MATERIALS: No special materials are required

GAME PROCEDURE: A member is selected and instructed by the leader (away from the group) to go into the center of the group and "Act like a _____." Group members are then encouraged to guess what or who the member is acting like and raise their hands if they know.
Some suggested situations are "Act like:

1. a person driving a car."

2. a swimmer."

3. making a bed."

4. mopping the floor."

5. eating a meal."

6. cooking a meal."

7. drawing a picture."

8. combing hair."

9. taking a shower."

PARTICIPATION
PROCEDURE: The BLIND SELECTION METHOD is used until all members have had a turn.

SUGGESTIONS: A more advanced version may involve the selection of two members who participate in cooperative role plays. Possible role-plays include throwing and catching a ball, playing cards, dancing, carrying something large, talking on the phone to each other.

TITLE: "What Am I Dressed For?"

SOCIALIZATION
GOAL AREA: Social competence

MATERIALS: (1) magazine pictures, sketches, written descriptions of situations suggested below; (2) clothing that goes with situations suggested below

GAME PROCEDURE: A group member selects one of the stimulus cards and identifies the situation. The member then chooses clothing appropriate to the situation depicted on the card. Group members vote "weird" or "OK" with respect to the appropriateness of the clothing.
Possible situations include:

1. Bed

2. Party

3. Work

4. School

5. Leisure time, e.g., walking, swimming

PARTICIPATION
PROCEDURE: The BLIND SELECTION METHOD is used.

SUGGESTIONS: The game may be made more advanced by having other group members (1) correct a "weird" match or (2) select another appropriate match.

TITLE: "Who Can Help?"

SOCIALIZATION
GOAL AREA: Social competence

MATERIALS: Index cards with magazine pictures
and titles of helpers such as policeman,
fireman, staff person, case manager,
social worker, work supervisor, friend,
etc.; box of containers with problem
situations on slips of paper

GAME PROCEDURE: A member selects a problem situation
from the problem box and then must
pick the appropriate helper from the
index cards.
Possible problems include:

1. You see a house on fire.

2. You are lost in the community.

3. You don't know how to do your job.

4. You didn't get your SSI check.

5. Your wallet was stolen.

6. You lost your money.

7. You want to go to a movie with someone.

8. You want to learn how to take the bus.

9. You need a job.

10. You want to talk to someone.

PARTICIPATION
PROCEDURE: The BLIND SELECTION METHOD
is used.

SUGGESTIONS: A leader may want to simplify the game
by limiting the number of helpers to
two or three specific to the accessibility
of group members, institutional or
community.

TITLE: "Don't Lose Your Cool" I

SOCIALIZATION
GOAL AREA: Social competence

MATERIALS: No special materials are required

GAME PROCEDURE: One member is selected to participate with the leader in an enactment which shows either a "cool" or "uncool" way to respond to a particular situation. The group is prompted to respond to the situation with the proper rating e.g. "He/she was cool" or "He/she lost lost his/her cool."

Role enactments:

1. One member teases the other.

2. One member takes something from the other.

3. One member threatens the other with a gesture.

4. One member calls the other a name.

5. One member grabs the other.

6. One member talks without listening to the other.

7. One member bumps into the other.

PARTICIPATION
PROCEDURE: The BLIND SELECTION METHOD is used.

SUGGESTIONS: The leader will initially want to participate as the responder to the incident while instructing the member as to his/her role. Nonverbal members may be encouraged to rate the response with a "thumbs-up" or "thumbs-down" gesture.

BIBLIOGRAPHY

Bendekovic, John. *Working with a Group.* Washington: The United States Justice Department (Grant # 1491-00-F1-71), 1971.

Edmonson, Barbara, Moxley, David, and Nevil, Nevalyn. Continued Development and Demonstration of a Program for Disturbed Retarded Institutional Residents. Final report of service development project FY 79 #00474, Ohio Department of Mental Health and Mental Retardation, Division of Mental Retardation and Developmental Disabilities. Columbus, Ohio: The Nisonger Center, The Ohio State University, 1980.

Edmonson, Barbara, Nevil, Nevalyn, and Moxley, David. "Developing Responsible Self Directed Behavior." 27-minute videotape cassette. Columbus, Ohio: The Nisonger Center, The Ohio State University, 1980.

Han, Sung Soon. Use of Socialization Games to Increase Prosocial Behavior of Institutionalized Retarded Women. Unpublished doctoral dissertation. The Ohio State University, 1980.

Moxley, David, Nevil, Nevalyn, and Edmonson, Barbara: "Meeting Time: Structured Group Activities with the Mentally Retarded." 27-minute videotape cassette. Columbus, Ohio: The Nisonger Center, The Ohio State University, 1980.

Nevil, Nevalyn and Edmonson, Barbara. "A Visit to a Group Home." 7-minute sychronized sound 35 mm slide show. Columbus, Ohio: The Nisonger Center, The Ohio State University, 1980.

Rosen, Marvin, Clark, Gerald R., and Kivitz, Marvin S. *Habilitation of the Handicapped.* Baltimore: University Park Press, 1977.

Rosen, Marvin and Hoffman, M. *Personal Adjustment Training,* Vol. III. *Appropriate Behavior Training: A Group Counseling Manual for the Mentally Handicapped.* Elwyn, Pennsylvania: The Elwyn Institute, 1975.

116

INDEX

117